Crisis at the Crossroads

by
Carlton Pearson

Dmetrius Publishing
Tulsa, OKlahoma

Over 18,000 in print

Crisis at the Crossroads
ISBN 0-89274-552-5
Copyright © 1989 by Carlton Pearson
P. O. Box 700007
Tulsa, Oklahoma 74170

Published by Dmetrius Publishing
P. O. Box 700007
Tulsa, Oklahoma 74170

Contents

Preface:

A Changing of the Seasons

For two years the Church of Jesus Christ has been at a crossroads — a transition from one spiritual season to another, or a changing of the guard. Church history shows us that any such time is a state of crisis. We are in a state of crisis.

The last such crisis was in the mid-Twenties when the Church was at a crossroads of decision as to its role in public affairs. There were attacks by the media then as there are now. Certain leaders fell, and "scandals" surfaced about others, while various factions within the Church seemed to turn on one another.

Whether we feel the Church in this country handled the Twenties' crisis rightly or not, we passed the crossroads, and God's purpose for His people never changed. He knows the end from the beginning. He has already won!

I am sharing in this book the things the Lord has shown me about the present crisis — the shaking of the Church that has been going on for more than two years. I am writing this for the sake of individuals — so that they can see what the Lord is doing and not wander off in the wrong direction from the crossroads. After pondering these things for more than twelve years, I have finally been released by God to share them in print.

Some of the things I say may make you uncomfortable. However, this is not really a time to be comfortable — this is a time to weep between the porch and the altar. (Joel 2:17, *King James Version*.)

Another way to use the word *crisis* is as a turning point in the progress of a disease. It seems God must bring these crises or crossroads in order to shake out certain "diseases" of the world that attack His Body. After such a crisis in the natural, a doctor can tell whether the patient is going to live or die. The difference in the spiritual realm is that after God's crises, His Body *always* lives and continues to grow.

It is not my purpose to identify the many different things which, like spiritual AIDS, have attacked the Church's immune system. But I feel God has given me not only permission but a mandate to examine the causes of the tensions and conditions that feed these "diseases."

My purpose is to show that this crisis — which has shaken so many in the religious world — is a divine turning point, a transition ordered by God and orchestrated by the Holy Spirit to prepare the Church for the greatest revival of holiness, joy, and power God's people have ever known — God's latter rain.

My prayer is that you will read these pages with an open mind and receive the message with an open heart. I pray the effect of this book on readers will be to cause, first of all, shepherds, and secondly, the sheep, to examine their lifestyles, attitudes, and behavior toward God and toward each other and to set their houses in order.

The spirit of Elijah is present in God's Church today, and many *are* hearing the voice of prophecy in the inner recesses of their spirits. There is a sensing of God's imminent return, first in latter rain and blessing, then in His return to catch away a spotless, blemish-less, and wrinkle-less *holy* Church.

The theme of this book is *the rain of the Holy Spirit.* In God's timing and by the sovereign design of His own calendar, *revival is coming* and His latter rain *will* fall.

Carlton Pearson

Tulsa, Oklahoma

Introduction:
It's Gonna Rain!

Ask the Lord for rain in the springtime; it is the Lord who makes the storm clouds.

He gives showers of rain to men, and plants of the field to everyone.

Zechariah 10:1

The changing of the seasons can be dramatic, a time of crisis, in the spiritual realm as well as in the natural world.

The "rains and waters" of the Holy Spirit are absolutely imperative to keep us spiritually free and clean from the toxic poisons of sin that enter our spiritual blood streams from the world's systems. Today, we badly need the rain of the Holy Spirit to wash away toxins of the world from the Body of Christ. We need spiritual rain even more than we need natural rain. However, the storms that bring the rain sometimes make people uncomfortable.

Knowing God's Times and Seasons

Times and seasons have a lot to do with when the rains come. Daniel 2:21 says, **He changes *times and seasons*; he sets up kings and deposes them.** In the context of the subject of this book, that passage could be interpreted this way: "He raises up ministries of leadership in His Church, and He allows other ministries or leaderships to expire or be decreased."

Praying *in* the will of God and moving in His timing is a discerning grace that many Christians must somehow appropriate in their lives. We must first hear the voice of God (that still, small voice) and then move into prayer and intercession. The purpose is not to bring about the promise or the prophecy already given, but to ensure our participation in that prophetic promise.

Like Jacob, some may sleep through the visitation, only to wake up and proclaim, "Surely the Lord is in this place, and I was not aware of it." (Gen. 28:16.)

All of this shaking in the Church of late has been a sign to me of the gathering of the storm clouds on the horizon, and a sign that something remarkable and incredible is about to burst forth on the Church. Whether it appears as a monsoon season of destructive storms and floods causing calamity and devastation in our lives, or *whether we perceive it as showers of spiritual blessings,* depends on *prayer* and on *hearing* God. But something definitely is going on!

Something Is Missing

One of the things that has distressed me for ten to fifteen years is the conspicuous absence of the power of God in the ways that we all know God is capable of manifesting Himself. We read of things that happened in the past, but very rarely do those things seem to be happening today.

The Holy Spirit has directed my attention to a similar situation in the time of Elijah. During the days of the greatest idolatry in the nation of Israel, God raised up Elijah as His answer to Ahab and Jezebel.

Jezebel was a demon incarnate, one of the nastiest spirits in Biblical history, one who harassed God's people and dared to strip their nation of their worship and devotion to Him. Ahab was derelict in his responsibilities and allowed Jezebel to move the focus of the nation from the Creator to the works of the flesh.

The works of the flesh (the Jezebel spirit) are conspicuous in the Church today, causing men and women to bow to idol worship. The "Ahabs," those placed in office to lead the Church, have allowed Satan to change the focus from the Creator to man's works. Whether it is denominations, church leaders and leading ministers, or doctrines that have been made into sacred cows — *it is all idol worship!*

We have worshipped our buildings, projects, and plans. And as you can see, all over the Body of Christ, God is shaking buildings, projects, and plans, as well as ministries, ministers, and denominations.

No Dew or Rain

First Kings 17:1 states:

> **Now Elijah the Tishbite, from Tishbe in Gilead, said to Ahab, As the Lord, the God of Israel, lives, whom I serve, there will be neither dew nor rain in the next few years except at my word.**

The lack of rain in the summer of 1988 was, I believe, a reflection in the natural of a lack of the Holy Spirit's influence in our lives spiritually and in our country. That was the hottest and dryest summer on record. Brush fires burned out of control all across this nation destroying millions of acres of forests and grasslands. Because of the lack of moisture (dew or rain) rivers and lakes fell to record lows causing plants and animals to die. Canals and channels became so shallow that fresh-water barges were unable to pass through the inland waterways with their cargo.

All of those things, I believe, were signs in the natural of happenings in the spiritual realm. God is trying to say something to His people — not just to those in America, but to His worldwide Church.

A sick and weak Church produces a sick and weak society.

A strong and productive Church produces a strong and productive society.

I believe the prophetic word of the Lord is saying there will be no move of the Holy Spirit — no dew or rain — *except at the word of His prophets.* In a spiritual sense, it will be the same as when Elijah said there would not be rain until he called for rain. (1 Kings 17:1.)

Several times I have found myself asking, "God, when is this drought going to be over? Won't it be soon?"

And He has answered, "It will rain again, but I'm not through yet."

When Will the Crisis End?

I have often said, "Lord, I don't want to talk about the famine any more. I feel like a 'prophet of doom and gloom.' Tell me, God, when will this crisis pass? When will we be past the crossroads?"

God answers, "When my people bow before me with broken hearts and contrite spirits. They are running around here and there looking for quick and easy answers, but not enough of My people want to hear My whole counsel. Preachers are making up things to tell the people."

God spoke to His people Israel through Jeremiah, saying:

> "Therefore," declares the Lord, "I am against the prophets who steal from one another words supposedly from me. Yes," declares the Lord, "I am against the prophets who wag their own tongues and yet declare, 'The Lord declares.' Indeed, I am against those who prophesy false dreams," declares the Lord. "They tell them and lead my people astray with their reckless lies, yet I did not send or appoint them. They do not benefit these people in the least," declares the Lord.
>
> Jeremiah 23:30-32

I believe God is speaking similar things to His people today.

Once I asked, "God, how can You allow the secular media to pounce upon us like they have? How can You permit the world to embarrass, expose, and humiliate Your people? How can You allow them to call what a few are doing a 'holy war' when in reality, it is the most 'unholy war' of this century? When is it going to end?"

God said:

> "When (not if) I shut up the heavens so that there is no rain (drought), or command locusts to devour the land (famine) or send a plague among my people (disease, perhaps AIDS), if my people, who are called by my name, will humble

> themselves and pray and seek my face and turn
> from their wicked ways, then will I hear from
> heaven and will forgive their sin and will heal
> their land."
>
> 2 Chronicles 7:13,14

God spoke those words to the young King Solomon after His glorious dedication of the first Temple. The construction of a "house" for the Lord had taken seven years, and the Lord had assisted Solomon's efforts. Eventually, however, the king and the people fell into pride, disobedience to the Word, and carelessness about hearing God. They forgot that the beauty and grandeur of the temple and Solomon's achievement in building it were attributable to God. In Second Chronicles 7:14, God pointed out where the responsibility for the consequences of disobedience rested:

If my people — not the government, the judicial systems, the bureaucracy of the social welfare system, but God's people — are the ones whose turning away from God caused the drought and famine. And God's people today, the Church of Jesus Christ, can — under a prophetic anointing of prayer and repentance — cause the rain of the Holy Spirit to fall again.

Are you hearing this in your spirit? *We* can bring back the glory from the cloudless skies!

Turn From Your Wicked Ways

Somehow God is going to turn what has been happening for His good and for our good. The devil means it for evil, and he has won a few battles. But he is not going to win the war. God is allowing the heat and pressure to be applied to iron out the blemishes, spots, and wrinkles in the Body of Christ.

We blame the media, Congress, the Supreme Court, and the President for the ills of society, but God does not name any of those.

He said *we* need to humble ourselves and pray — not the government or the world. I believe we are humbling ourselves and seeking His face, but *we are not yet turning from our wicked ways.* The Bible says that in the days of Elijah, the people were worshipping the Lord and *serving their own gods* at the same time. I believe that is what we are doing.

Revival is always preceded by humbling and repentance. If God's people truly repent, *then* we will see a great revival. Right now, we are in the days of "neither dew nor rain," and I believe God has special instructions for His people just as He had for Elijah.

The Lord said to Elijah, "Leave here."

He was saying, "It is not going to rain, and there is going to be a famine, so leave here."

In other words, He said, *"Move from where you are and follow My Spirit."*

A Christian's question today should be the same as Elijah's, "Well, Lord, where do I go?"

Find the Place of Separation

The Lord told Elijah to go toward the east and drink from the brook of Kerith, and He would send ravens to feed him. (1 Kings 17:2.) *Kerith* means "a cutting away." To us, the Kerith Ravine is a place of separation, a place of cutting away the flesh, hiding away from the famine and being fed by the Lord. There Elijah would be supplied with both water (anointing) and meat (the Word).

Some of us do not want to stay in the ravine. We want to go there and pass through. But Elijah had to stay there for months. We want to pass through the ravine quickly because it is lonely there. There are not many folks in there with us. The flesh has to die there. There is no room for pride, self-will, or lust in that hiding place, but it is the only place we can receive nourishment during the spiritual famine.

I believe this is what God is saying to us today: "Find that secret place in Me. Do not fight the media or fight one another. Get somewhere on your face before Me. It is time to begin to weep, pray, and fast."

After Elijah had been in the ravine for some time, even the brook of Kerith dried up because of the lack of rain, and the Lord sent him somewhere else. (v. 7.) When God moves you out of the "cutting away place" because the brook dries up, you have to go to a place of refinement.

First, God is going to cut away all the junk and dross, all the lying and flesh, every weight and sin that so easily besets us, then we are going to that place called "Zarephath" where He will refine, or define, our ministries and our lives. (See vv. 8-16.)

Now is not the time to leave the place where God is watering you, wherever it is. If you are being fed in the midst of this famine — stay there. But if you are trying to drink from a dry hole, you had better move on. Find out where God is moving, and if you cannot find such a place, let Him move in you — and then you start to move! If you will do that, you can really stand in these days of the shaking of the Lord. However, we need to remember the Lord promises that after He unleashes judgments, He will restore *if His people repent and turn.*

Do you hear what I hear?

First Kings 18:1,41-45 KJV states:

> And it came to pass after many days, that the word of the LORD came to Elijah in the third year, saying, Go, shew thyself unto Ahab; and I will send rain upon the earth.
>
> And Elijah said unto Ahab, Get thee up, eat and drink; for there is a sound of abundance of rain.
>
> So Ahab went up to eat and to drink, And Elijah went up to the top of Carmel; and he cast himself down upon the earth, and put his face between his knees,
>
> And said to his servant, Go up now, look toward the sea. And he went up, and looked, and said, There is nothing. And he said, Go again seven times.
>
> And it came to pass at the seventh time, that he said, Behold, there ariseth a little cloud out of the sea, like a man's hand. And he said, Go up, say unto Ahab, Prepare thy chariot, and get thee down, that the rain stop thee not.
>
> And it came to pass in the meanwhile, that the heaven was black with clouds and wind, and there was a great rain. And Ahab rode, and went to Jezreel.

Do you *see* what I hear?

That cloud is on the horizon, seemingly insignificant to many, but nonetheless there. The rain is coming, it is on the holy horizon. A great revival is truly on the way, but several things must occur first.

It *will* rain again, my friend, but the climate and the season must be right — both in the world and in each of our hearts. In *my* heart, I do hear the sound of the abundance of rain, the sound of a time of refreshing.

1
Do You See What I Hear?

This is a prophetic book, and I want you to read it in that frame of mind.

I have tried to have as positive an attitude as I can. I am trying to believe God for the best, but this is the hardest word the Lord has ever given me to deliver. Before, when He had me preach about "sin in the camp," it was to bring repentance so there would be no major disasters in judgment. But this time, He has shown me judgment is already upon us, and that it is part of a transition He is orchestrating by His own providence and will.

I said, "Lord, you mean there is nothing we can do? Why are you even telling me if there is nothing we can do?"

He said, "I want you to warn the people so they will not be discouraged as it happens. But tell them *not to even mourn about it*. Tell them to trust Me and keep moving forward."

Our hope as Christians must be in the fact that God *will* have His kingdom on earth as it is in heaven (Matt. 6:10), and that He will have a holy people. We must learn that God's unconditional love for us does not mean unconditional permissiveness. A loving parent is not one who allows his child free reign to do as he pleases, but one who spares not the rod in order to develop self-control and self-discipline in his child.

The Word says God chastens and rebukes those He loves. (Rev. 3:19.) Our hope must be in the fact that His love is being expressed in this shaking of the Church. He loves us too much not to correct us.

Therefore, in spite of the hard things I have seen and that I foresee, my hope is in the love and mercy of my Lord, and I am grateful that He cares enough for us to clean us up. I hope every reader of this book will be similarly encouraged.

A Divine Crossroads

We are coming to a divine intersection or crossroads in the history of the church. And all of us need to find our places in what God is doing. We will have security and a better sense of direction if we understand where we are in history. It should encourage each of us greatly to know that God has called us at such a time. *Something is about to happen.* However, in order to know what God is doing, we have to be able to hear Him.

The first thing most of us do when we get out of bed or get home from somewhere is turn on the television or radio. I used to flip on the television just for the sound as soon as I walked into a hotel room.

Then one day the Lord said, "Shut that thing off. I want to talk to you. You cannot hear Me when you are listening to everything else."

Shut down everything else, and listen to God. He wants to speak to you personally. He wants a personal romance with you. The only way to keep your nourishment in these times is to get shut in with God.

People are dying from little twenty-minute sermons with three points and a poem. They are in famine in many churches. In other churches, they are dying of the letter of the law. I do not care how good the sermon is, if there is no anointing and the Holy Spirit is not moving, it will kill you. There is no rain in it. All this unanointed, dry preaching is killing people.

Our ministries have lost definition. Our churches do not know why they exist. We think they exist to raise money, to start programs, to have bazaars — as an end in themselves. But most of them have become as spiritually pale as the weak tea, as cold as the ice cream, and as dead as the chicken served up at church suppers.

You need to find a little brook somewhere as Elijah did. It may not be the biggest, finest church around, but it better be where the life of God is, where the water of the Spirit can be found.

The Bible says the Word of God is sharper than a two-edged sword, that it pierces even to the dividing of soul and spirit, joints and marrow. (Heb. 4:12.) The bone structure and the marrow of the Church is diseased because not enough of the Word that is quick and powerful is being put forth. Get enough of the Word, and lying is cut out. Deceitfulness is cut out. Lust and pride are cut out. God is doing surgery on His Church with a two-edged sword. His sword is in His hand.

What Causes Famine?

Famine in the Bible was caused by one of four things: An absence of rain (drought), a plague of locusts or caterpillars, a seizing of the land or the water supply by the enemy.

We sing the song, "Blow the Trumpet in Zion," and have no idea what it means. That is not a rejoicing song from the book of Joel. Those verses are a song of alarm. When the prophet talked about locusts rushing on the city and climbing up the walls, he was not talking about God's people. He was speaking about a plague of devouring locusts that God, in His warnings of coming judgment, had unleashed upon Israel's encampments.

> **Blow the trumpet in Zion; sound the alarm on my holy hill. Let all who live in the land tremble, for the day of the Lord is coming. It is close at hand —.**
>
> **Joel 2:1**

The army of locusts that the prophet Joel was using as a picture of spiritual things was very real to the people of his day. The Bible was written by men who lived in the deserts and understood the terrible damage of locusts. The insects flew in droves, like the rushing, violent wind of the desert. They came like a dark cloud of blackness no one could stop or protect their crops from. They devoured any and everything in their way.

Sounds like the media today, does it not? I am tired of the media reporting to me what is happening in my "family." What they are reporting is not what God is doing. They are the locusts, rushing on the city of God and running on the wall.

Preachers are being embarrassed. The Internal Revenue Service is scrutinizing ministries. Preachers are running from exposure. Even politicians are running. That is a sign in the natural of what God is doing in the spiritual. He is rolling back the curtain on sin. He is disclosing hidden sin. Man or woman of God, clean up your life, so there is nothing to hide!

You are going to see unspiritual leaders who pull the wool over the eyes of people, rob them of their money and faith, and lie to them eaten up with dread diseases, diseases with no known cause or cure.

You are going to see people drop dead in churches as they did in the days of Ananias and Sapphira. (Acts 5.) I am talking about "graveyard dead," funeral and flowers dead. You are going to see them suddenly, tragically — and some of them seemingly prematurely — removed from their positions. You are going to clearly see the drought that results from judgment, with its accompanying famine.

Some of us have heard the love of God preached so long that we forget what can happen when the Church is being shaken. Sometimes your ministry, or your bank account, or your marriage will die, if those things are not committed to God.

If this happens, He is warning you that *you* are next in line. You had better get things under the blood. You have no protection outside that. Find the brook.

The Stars No Longer Shine

Before them the earth shakes, the sky trembles, the sun and moon are darkened, and the stars no longer shine.

Joel 2:10

Those who were stars out in front with everyone looking at them have fallen. Christian celebrities no longer shine. They have lost their illumination (the light of God), and they have lost the artificial light of the world. Now they are standing in the shadow of darkness instead of the shadow of God. Churches that have been on the front pages of magazines as shining stars are losing their luster. It is a sobering time.

But we should not get mad at the news media or the church leaders who have been exposed. It is time to get on our knees. We are not illegitimate children with no father. We have a father who is parenting us right now. The Body of Christ is getting a whipping. Sometimes Jesus has to go through the Temple with a whip in His hands. *But the same hand that hits will heal when we repent on our knees and ask His forgiveness.*

One more time, I want to tell you: General assemblies, councils, convocations, associations, fellowships, and denominational gatherings are going to be judged. God began with the spiritual leadership, because if He let us go on the way we were headed, all of us would end up in hell.

The Church is not supposed to be an object of scorn. When the world points its finger at us, it is supposed to be because we are healing the sick and casting out devils or shutting down bars, taverns, and abortion clinics. Let them point their fingers at us because we live holy and love one another, not because of our conspicuous sin.

The city of Zarephath was in Sidon, which means "hunting place." If there ever was a time to become a huntsman of God, it is now. Hunt God, not Christian stars.

Jim and Tammy Bakker did not go to Calvary for you. Oral Roberts, Billy Graham, Robert Schuller, Kenneth Hagin, Pat Robertson, Paul Crouch, and other men, no matter how spiritual or righteous, did not go to Calvary for you.

Their blood does not atone for your sin. Only the blood of Jesus.

Not too long ago, I began to really hear something that has been said by television and radio evangelists, teachers, and preachers for years. I have even said it myself. It is this: "If you have a need, if you have a problem, if you want to be saved or healed, call me. Go to your phone and call me."

Now I know what we all meant by that. Nevertheless, we are not the saviors, healers, and deliverers. But we have made the people too dependent on going to that phone. I understand people need to acknowledge their commitment to Christ, but the Bible says there is *one mediator* between God and man. That mediator is Jesus. Somehow we have got to redirect the attention of the people to Jesus.

We can also learn lessons for today from the book of Ezekiel. The theme of the book is this: *to know that God is God.* Sixty-two times, in twenty-seven of the forty-eight chapters, the Lord says, **And they shall know that I am the Lord** (Ez. 6:10 KJV). Today, God is calling the Church back to a new focus upon Who is really Lord.

Whenever there has been a great outpouring of the Holy Spirit, that move always has been preceded

25

by "earthquakes," the shaking judgments of God, so you had better get ready.

The Shaking Is for Our Good

The shaking is for our good and for the good of the Lord's purposes. Judgment is occurring because the Church has turned away from those purposes. Yes, a lot has happened in the last couple of years, and perhaps a lot more will come, but we need not mourn as some would expect. We must move on in God, lick our wounds, and press toward that mark of His high calling. God has His hand on us, and we are still His chosen people.

2
This Is No Time to Mourn

The world is being shaken as well as the Church. There is AIDS; there are nuclear threats, famines, droughts, fires out of control, and so forth. We have killer bees, killer ants, and killer grasshoppers. The dairy industry is threatened with poison pollutants. Farmers are quaking under economic onslaughts. The oil industry has been shaken. Oklahoma was at one time a very proud and wealthy state; now it is economically very depressed. Tulsa at one time was the wealthiest city in the nation, per capita, with more than eleven hundred millionaires. Today, that number has decreased considerably.

Not long ago, about 5 a.m. the Lord woke me up and sent me to these scriptures:

> "Son of man, with one blow I am about to take away from you the delight of your eyes. Yet do not lament or weep or shed any tears. Groan quietly; do not mourn for the dead. Keep your turban fastened and your sandals on your feet; do not cover the lower part of your face or eat the customary food of mourners."
>
> So I spoke to the people in the morning, and in the evening my wife died. The next morning I did as I had been commanded.
>
> Ezekiel 24:16-18

Ezekiel's wife is not mentioned any other time in the Bible, but obviously he adored her, because the

Lord called her the delight of Ezekiel's eyes. However, at her passing, *God would not even permit Ezekiel to mourn.* He was to carry on as if nothing had happened *as a sign to the Jews who had been carried off into Babylon.*

> Then the people asked me, "Won't you tell us what these things have to do with us?"
>
> So I said to them, "The word of the Lord came to me: Say to the house of Israel (which means the Church in our day), 'This is what the Sovereign Lord says: I am about to desecrate my sanctuary — the stronghold in which you take pride, the delight of your eyes, the object of your affection. The sons and daughters you left behind will fall by the sword.'
>
> And you will do as I have done. You will not cover the lower part of your face or eat the customary food of mourners. You will keep your turbans on your heads and your sandals on your feet. You will not mourn or weep but will waste away because of your sins and groan among yourselves. Ezekiel will be a sign to you; you will do just as he has done. When this happens, you will know that I am the Sovereign Lord.'"
>
> Ezekiel 24:19-24

Letting God Be God

The prophet's wife died — but it was not judgment upon her or upon the prophet. Her death was for the sake of the nation of Judah. The ten and a half tribes of the nation of Israel had been carried off more than one hundred years before by Assyrians. The only Israelites left were those remaining in the land of Judah and those who were carried off to Babylon, who began to be called Jews after this time.

The Jews in exile were those to whom Ezekiel was prophesying in these verses.

Ezekiel's *wife*, in this context, also stands for the thing to which you are committed. The Jews were committed to their country, but not wholeheartedly to God. They worshipped God, but they also worshipped idols. So at this time God was in the process of allowing His people to be humiliated while the whole world watched. He allowed the land, the nation, and the temple — which had become a house for idols (Ezek. 8) and an object of pride — to be removed from them *to try to get their hearts and minds focused back on Him.*

Scripture shows that this kind of shaking and exile is only done by God as a last resort and only after many years of pleading, exhorting, and warning through his prophets.

As I saw this the morning God wakened me, my heart began to pound as He showed me the Church is first of all to be humbled, then the things that we have deified and idolized as our dearest delights are going to be taken from us with one blow. God is going to purge the Church. This can happen on a personal level as well.

During the captivity, the remnant of Judah was purged and cured permanently of worshipping natural idols. In the spiritual sense, idolatry can be of money, possessions, a spouse, and so forth. But never again did the Jews make offerings to statues of demons or wear amulets and talismans, nor did they deal in any of the idolatry you see today in places such as India and other Eastern countries.

I hate to say this, but in the midst of this wonderful Charismatic renewal, the Church has slipped into a form of idolatry. We idolize ministries, buildings, projects and programs, and doctrines. We have become an idolatrous generation. We teach things the world teaches. We prize and revere success in the form of money and possessions. We mimic and pattern ourselves after the world, and God has had all He can take.

Even in the birth of this new, coming move of the Holy Spirit, the world will try to embrace, caress, fondle, and rape the Church. (Ezek. 23:5-9.) We must learn to be different. The Church *must* stand out from the world. Even in Christian colleges and universities and in Christian businesses, there is as much sin as in the world. I have heard very embarrassing things about ministries that I believed in and about Christian businesses or Christian businessmen!

During the early days of the shaking of Judah, the Lord sent three great prophets to tell the people clearly what He was doing:

Jeremiah was preaching in Jerusalem. Ezekiel was in the hill country of Judah and later with the captives in Babylon. And Daniel was carried off as a very young man with the first wave of captivity and prophesied thereafter in Babylon. All three of those great ministries called the Jews to repentance, but Judah did not repent any more than Israel had a century before.

No Pentecost Before Repentance

Look at America today, a country that has been a symbol of Christianity to the world. We have had great revivals and many warnings from God. But in the past few decades, America has been plagued by horrible diseases, financial trouble, disasters and catastrophes, and scandals in the secular and the church world.

Crime is on the increase, especially "white-collar" crime. The Lord spoke to me that "white-collar" crime is a lot worse than "blue-collar" crime, because corporate crime can affect an entire city's welfare as opposed to the welfare of a single individual.

Most men and women of God have not committed crimes, but many have abused their anointings and neglected their stewardship of the gifts that operate through them. Now entire ministries are in terrible trouble. Their "wives," the delights of their lives, are crumbling before their eyes. Suddenly in one blow, the things that were the delight of their lives and the pride of their eyes are being taken from them — and there is more to come.

Something Powerful Is on the Way

God is going to humble us, and *then* the great revival is coming. Everyone is talking about the great harvest, the great revival, the great new move of the Holy Spirit, but there will be no Pentecost before repentance and cleansing. The Church is going to be sanctified and purged, and you might as well get ready for it. Something powerful is breaking loose.

Ministers are now fabricating miracles. They are making stuff up. They are saying they heard from God when they did not hear from God. They are saying God spoke to them when He did not speak to them. They are acting as if they have a prophetic word from God, but God is not in it.

He said to Elijah when Elijah hid in the cave that He (God) was not in that fire and not in that wind; He was not even in that earthquake. He was just passing by. The only reason for the fire and wind and earthquake was that He was passing by. (1 Kings 19:11-18.)

We have been proud of our whirlwind achievements, our great earthshaking revelations, and our powerful fire falling down because of walking in faith — but Jesus is still just passing by. He did not stay there. Wherever He passes by, however, something is going to happen.

God has blessed the Body of Christ today more than ever before. He has blessed Christian ministries. We have satellite hookups. We are on television and radio twenty-four hours a day. There are conventions, conferences, and seminars. It seems as if the fire is falling, the wind is blowing, and there is an earthquake. But God is not in it. He may be *for* it, but He is not necessarily *in* it. He is in that still small voice, that gentle whisper, and we have to get back to that secret place in Him in order to hear Him.

Some of us are hanging around the fire that fell, the wind that blew, and the earth that shook, *but God is passing on down the road*. He is moving on to another dimension, a holier road, and we had better get behind Him and follow Him all the way. The prophet's wife is about to die. Some "wives" already have.

"'I the Lord have spoken. The time has come for me to act. I will not hold back; I will not have pity, nor will I relent. You will be judged according to your conduct and your actions, declares the Sovereign Lord.'"

Ezekiel 24:14

God has been patient, let things happen, and tolerated sin to His limit. He has pleaded with us just as He did with Israel and Judah. All kinds of fires, winds, and shakings have occurred, but we have not listened any more than they did. The Body of Christ is going to experience spiritual AIDS if we do not stop what we are doing. Our immune system is shutting down. We have been overly careless.

Spiritual Adultery and Idolatry Go Together

Look at Ezekiel 22:30,31:

"I looked for a man among them who would build up the wall and stand before me in the gap on behalf of the land so I would not have to destroy it, but I found none. So I will pour out my wrath on them and consume them with my fiery anger, bringing down on their own heads all they have done, declares the Sovereign Lord."

God was not talking to sinners. He was talking to the Israelites in Judah, the believers. He was talking to saints. And today, He is speaking this to the Church. In the Ezekiel 23, God used the analogy of two sisters who were His, but later went into adultery and prostitution to other gods. The "two sisters" were Israel and Judah, the two nations into which the Israelites had split after the death of King Solomon.

Spiritual adultery and idolatry go hand in hand. The Israelites living in Judah loved and idolized the temple, although at that time, they were even worshipping idols *in* the temple. That is why God said He would desecrate it (which *they* already had) and even destroy it.

Today, God finds us in love with our "temples," yet worshipping the idols of Mammon within them (money, success, and power). We are into the idolatry of "Who can build the biggest church building or complex? Who can get the most members?" But we are not glorifying Jesus as we should. We think in America that we have "a corner on the market" of the Word. But God is going to shake all that out of us. People are deifying their own ministries more than Jesus.

Look how far God has brought the Church. There are Christians in the U. S. Congress, in the Supreme Court, and in other high places. God has blessed the Church, but if we get uplifted in pride, we are going to lose our idols. The strongholds in which we take pride, the delights of our eyes, the objects of our affections will be taken from us.

The sons and daughters you left behind (in Judah when the parents were taken into captivity) **will fall by the sword** (Ezek. 24:21).

Some of the baby Christians we are supposed to be nurturing are going to fall. We are going to lose them because we are so busy doing our own things that we are not caring for them. Some of these babies are coming in with the scent of the world on them. And we may lose them in this shaking, because we are so into ourselves that they can tell we do not *really* care about them. Even baby Christians can tell from the attitude and behavior of a ministry whether the people really care. They can go into a church and know whether the leaders there care about the people or about themselves and their own success.

The Little Foxes

I believe many ministers have lost their burden for the people. Their burden is for themselves and their name and image. Judgment has come, and the only way to escape it is to acknowledge the problem. What do you care about? Ministers, what do you love? Is it money, possessions, power, worldly success — or Jesus? What are you lusting for as the two "sisters" did? God says that if we love anything more than Him, we are not worthy of Him.

Pride says, "I have big things going. Glory to God, the money is rolling. I had faith, and I trusted God. Now I'm in charge."

That prideful arrogance is being stripped. God is coming back for a holy Church. Most of the sins of the Church are subtle. Most of us are not outward adulterers, murderers, and liars, but the **little foxes ... ruin the vineyards** (Song of Sol. 2:15). The little things that trigger pride and ego are the things to which we have to die.

Today, many ministers and Church leaders manipulate the sheep. They manipulate their own lives. Many of the shepherds and many sheep try to manipulate God as if He were a heavenly Santa Claus or a cosmic bellhop. We do not trust Him anymore. We just try to manipulate Him. That is the same thing the devil did in heaven and that is why he was cast out. He tried to manipulate and assert his authority over God.

The Israelites loved the milk and honey of the Promised Land, but they did not love God enough to obey His commandments and instructions. They loved the blessings, but did not walk in willingness and obedience to avoid the curses.

You have to love holiness in order to walk in it. We are losing our fervency in praise. When the Church was poor, it was humble, spiritual, and discerning. Now that we are prosperous, we are full of pride, and even envy and jealousy because God blessed someone else with a bigger car or a bigger church.

> **Pride goes before destruction, a haughty spirit before a fall.**
>
> **Proverbs 16:18**

I asked God if this really had to happen to us, and He said, "Ezekiel asked the same thing. Jeremiah asked the same thing."

God *Will* Clean Up His Church

He said that we are not going to escape this judgment. We are coming to a time of transition. Ministries are going to falter and churches collapse. Today they may be the biggest thing going, but tomorrow there may be nothing left of them. Secret sins are being revealed. And while this is sad and scary at the same time, it is a witness to me that God is going to clean up the ministries and the Church.

In this next wave, we are going to have the manifestations of the Holy Spirit operating through people who are walking in the Spirit and living holy. Holiness will seal you. It will lock you into the will of God, and you will flow under that divine anointing.

We are going to be able to attend services in days to come and say, "No evil have I done."

None of us really want to go into sin. The Holy Spirit in us hates it, but our flesh plays with the toys of pride and ego.

God is saying, "You keep fooling around with that, and I am going to turn you over to the thing you hate, to those you turned away from in disgust. They will deal with you in hatred and take away everything you have worked for."

We are going to have to carry on in the midst of all these shakings and judgments. We do not have time to stop and mourn and lament. God is shifting the leadership. There are going to be changes, but we must just carry on anyway.

When this happens, when "the wife" dies, people are going to have a new hunger for divine, unadulterated truth, unsugar-coated, unglamorized, and undiluted. They are going to say, "Tell us what is going on," when right now they do not want to hear the truth. They do not want to hear about judgments.

God seldom allows the destruction of His sanctuary, and when He does, it is because His people have already done so. But He is now allowing some ministries, churches and people to be destroyed before our eyes. When the people we put our hopes in are no longer there, the ministries we look up to are no longer in existence, the churches we thought were so great have Ichabod (which means "the glory has departed") written over their doors, those of us left must go on.

Isaiah said, **In the year that King Uzziah died, I saw the Lord** (Is. 6:1). And God said when this is all over, the Church is once again going to *see the Lord.* We are going to know that God is God.

Suppose we did not have camp meetings and beautiful places where Christians could congregate, could we live holy anyway? Can we have Jesus without all of the amenities? If there were no Christian television and radio, could we live holy? If there were no tape ministries, could we live holy? What will we do when the wind stops, the fire goes out, and the earth stops shaking? When Uzziah dies, will we see the Lord?

Will we have two wings to cover our faces in reverence to His holiness? Will we have two wings to cover our feet in humility? Will we have two wings to fly away and serve Jesus?

We are so into our own little things that we have lost the sound of what Jesus is saying. We are so busy riding the bicycle that Daddy bought us that we have forgotten that Daddy bought it. We think we deserve it because we said all the right things and did all the right things. Every time we get a blessing, it is grace. We cannot earn it. We do not deserve it. We ought to be glad and praise His name for everything.

We are not suffering as the early saints did. They are not feeding us to the wild animals and beasts. They are not stoning us to death. We are the most blessed Church in the history of the world, and every time we get something from God, we should be saying, "Thank You, Father," not "Look what I believed for and got." We need to change the word *believe* to the word *obey.*

If it sounds as if I am "down" on preachers, there are two reasons: 1) I *am* a preacher who is preaching to himself, and 2) God's judgments in the Bible always were first with the leadership, the shepherds, then with the sheep. God's first order of business in this shaking is dealing with His shepherds. We will talk about His dealings with the sheep later.

3
Woe to You, Shepherds

"Son of man, prophesy against the shepherds of Israel; prophesy and say to them: 'This is
what the Sovereign Lord says: *Woe to the shepherds* of Israel who only take care of themselves!
Should not shepherds take care of the flock?'"

Ezekiel 34:2

In Ezekiel 34, before God ever promised
showers of blessing (v. 26), he dealt rather harshly
with first the "shepherds" (vv. 1-16) and then with
the "sheep" (vv. 17-24). As I have prayerfully viewed
and reviewed the state of the Church as we approach
the end of the century, I am observing a similar
pattern to that recorded in Ezekiel 34.

I am sure you will agree that during 1987 and
1988, God's dealings with shepherds and/or spiritual
leadership has been quite obvious both to the secular
world and to the Church. Tearfully, I have asked God
many times why we must display our dirty laundry
before the world by washing it in the public
washeteria of mass-media scrutiny.

His reply was, "Because you do not wash your
dirty laundry yourselves in the privacy of your own
home utility rooms."

God has supplied every believer with his own
private room where he can wash the soiled garments
of his own spiritual wardrobe. There is a "laundry
room" in every heart. I am speaking of the utility

room of the soul, the place of repentance and forgiveness of sins.

When we do not take care of our dirty linen privately, God will do it publicly. If we will not bathe in seclusion, God will shout our uncleanness from the housetops — and that is exactly what He has been doing. Almost every antenna in every housetop in America has pulled our open rebuke into every room that has a working television set. Never before in the history of the Church have so many people jeered and laughed at the feuding families of faith.

The Root of the Problem

In verses 1-3 of Ezekiel 34, the prophet points immediately to the root of Israel's problem in his denunciation of the unspiritual attitudes and behavior of the religious leadership. I have seen in our day that strong and decisive spiritual leadership will produce "followship" after its own kind.

In verse two, Ezekiel says: **Woe to the shepherds ... who only take care of themselves**. Self-seeking, self-loving, self-centered leadership in the Church has been the curse of modern Christianity. From the boardrooms of denominational ecclesiastical hierarchies to the mailrooms of the largest or smallest para-church organizations across this world, we have seen the power of love perverted. The power of love perverted becomes the *love of power.*

God loves His people. He loves the Church, the spiritual Body of His Son and the physical expression of Himself in the world. He is concerned with their problems. He has acted in history and continues to act to meet our needs. Both political and religious institutions are supposed to exist for the benefit and well-being of people, but somehow, they have a tendency to become corrupt with time.

Human beings, although they are all God has to carry out His will in this earth, are inclined to pursue the lusts for power and personal ambitions inherent in the nature of fallen man. Even God's people often pursue these lusts to the detriment and misfortune of the very people whom they are called to serve.

Sometimes it is hard to decide whether the primary problems in the Church are a result of poor leadership or poor "followship"!

In Old Testament Israel, God used both kings and prophets to carry out His will in and through the nation. The prophets, representing spiritual leadership, were present in Israel long before the kings, who represented political leadership. Some of those in spiritual leadership remained dedicated to the Lord and served to balance out the progressive corruption of the political regimes. However, eventually the two began to mix roles, causing both political and spiritual degeneration. The same is almost the case today.

Five Things God Has Against Shepherds

In verses four and five, the Lord lists five things He has against the shepherds:

1. You have not strengthened the weak.

2. You have not healed the sick.

3. You have not bound up the injured.

4. You have not brought back the strays.

5. You have not sought for the lost.

When wolves or other predators attack a flock of sheep or herd of cattle, they first go after the very young, the very old, or the sick. The word *weak* as it is used here was translated in the *King James Version* as "diseased." The Hebrew meaning would better suggest "the sore," "the pained," or "the feeble or anemic."

In other words, *the weak* are those Christians who because of immaturity, the lack of proper nourishment, weariness from battle, or injury from war have become disfunctional or in any way incapacitated. In far too many churches, we ignore the ordinary people. If they do not have money, talent, or good looks, they are overlooked, disregarded, or manipulated.

God is not pleased with shepherds who cater only to the rich and powerful. Most church boards consist of the largest givers in the church, regardless of their lifestyles. Often those large givers are the most carnal, egotistical bigots in the congregation. They pounce on the humble, disregard the poor, and take advantage of the weak.

The second "you have not" is *you have not healed the sick*. The Hebrew meaning of the word *healed* as it is used here is "to mend" (by stitching), suggesting the repair of something torn, split, or broken. Literally, it would mean "to cure, or to make whole or complete" — not necessarily in the physical sense as in divine healing, but in a spiritual sense.

Galatians 6:1,2 says:

Brothers, if someone is caught in a sin, you who are spiritual should restore him gently. But watch yourself, or you also may be tempted. Carry each other's burdens, and in this way you will fulfill the law of Christ.

The Greek word used here for "sin" is *paraptoma*, which means "a slipping across," as on an icy road. The word has no meaning of deliberate sin but rather of an accidental stumbling on a dangerous or rocky path. The word *caught* in the first verse could have been paraphrased "trapped" or "ensnared."

Paul, then, is saying, "You who are spiritual, *restore* such a person."

Restore means "to repair or mend, to fix, or to make fit." One of the responsibilities of a shepherd is to function as a "restorer or repairer" of the brethren (saints). Some shepherds are so busy looking after their own concerns that they do not have the time, or they do not take the time, to "anoint the heads of the sheep with oil" as David said in Psalm 23.

Ministers have become too impatient and intolerant of sheep who are crippled mentally, emotionally, or physically. Many shepherds today love to build large buildings and big names for themselves, but they do not take the time to build souls for God. Life, even for Christians, is often burdensome and imposing. A godly shepherd is sensitive to that, and in loving pastoral care, he assists his sheep with all diligence and Christlike compassion. Galatians 6:2 says to **carry each other's burdens.**

The third "you have not" involves *binding up the injured.* The word *bind* means "to wrap firmly" as a turban or tourniquet to stop bleeding from an injury or an accident. Also, it could be an equivalent of putting on a cast or splint to set a broken bone to allow it to heal properly.

I do not remember when I have encountered more injured Christians nationwide than I have noticed during the past several years. Everywhere I go, there are broken hearts that cannot love or forgive. There are "broken legs and feet" that cripple, and in some cases paralyze, the spiritual walk of many saints. I have seen "broken arms" that are shortened and deformed, unable to reach up to God or out to man in love.

We shepherds must go to work prayerfully and lovingly to find those injured souls and to wrap them firmly in the love of God to stop this senseless bleeding and hemorrhaging of their faith. God help us to do that!

For the fourth thing God has against shepherds, *The King James Version* says, **Neither have ye brought again that which was driven away** (Ez. 34:4d). Notice the Lord did not say "stolen away." When we lose believers or church members to another church, denomination, or even to sin, we tend to blame it directly on the devil. Of course, Satan is ultimately in back of any loss in our lives — money, marriage, ministry, or otherwise. However, I think we have given him more "credit" than he deserves, or at least we have not accepted our rightful share of the blame. Some Christians stray from God and go back into the world. I am a pastor, and I have seen that happen. However, many "backslidden" Christians are the result of the pastor or someone in the congregation having "driven the sheep away."

The prophet used *driven* here in the sense of "to push off" or "to expel." A similar Greek word is used in the New Testament to describe the casting out of demons by Jesus. He "expelled" them. He ran them off; he chased them away. Jealousy, greed, competition, and prejudice literally have driven thousands of Christians into the arid plains of spiritual drought and famine where they have starved to death for lack of spiritual nourishment and love, or they are starving right now.

In John 10:11-13, the apostle quotes Jesus as saying:

> I am the good shepherd. The good shepherd lays down his life for the sheep. The hired hand is not the shepherd who owns the sheep. So when he sees the wolf coming, he abandons the sheep and runs away. Then the wolf attacks the flock and scatters it. The man runs away because he is *a hired hand* and cares nothing for the sheep.

When a hireling *sees* a wolf coming, he abandons the sheep. He runs from the responsibility of protecting or even warning the sheep. That kind of pastor is not a true shepherd. Any pastor who lets wolves, who often come dressed in sheep's clothing (Matt. 7:15), chase the sheep away from within the congregation is in the ministry for the wrong reason. He does not care for the sheep.

The fifth and last "you have not" is *you have not sought for the lost.* The figurative meaning of *sought* in the Hebrew is "to be broken-hearted for the lost." The word implies petitioning, requesting, even begging

47

vigorously or intently. Many shepherds today have lost the vision of world evangelization. Most try to reach "denomination quotas" through giving for missionary support, but the motivation is to receive recognition from "headquarters" or to impress their peers. The motive is too rarely the love of the lost.

Haggai 1:4 quotes the Lord as saying:

> **"Is it a time for you yourselves to be living in your paneled houses, while this house remains a ruin?"**

To apply that verse in a spiritual sense to today's Church, it would read, "Is this a time for you to be building elaborate and ostentatious cathedrals and churches while My spiritual house — *the* Church — lies in ruins?"

The lost souls of men are plunging into hell by the thousands every day, while God's shepherds are busy pridefully and carnally competing with each other, vying for the applause of men. In Matthew 18:12, Jesus made a reference to this kind of thing, which apparently also was occurring in His day. He said:

> **"What do you think? If a man owns a hundred sheep, and one of them wanders away, will he not leave the ninety-nine on the hills and go to look for the one who wandered off?"**

Somehow, the leaders of the Church, in general, have lost sight of the target and have become independent introverts — "Lone Rangers" — thinking only of themselves and their "paneled houses," and God is sorely displeased.

When the Rain Falls

My heart has been grieved, and if it were not for the promises in Ezekiel 34:25-31, I would truly be weeping as one who has no hope. But praise God, there *is* hope, and our joy can — and surely will — be restored one day.

I will bless them and the places surrounding my hill. I will send down showers in season; there will be showers of blessing.
Ezekiel 34:26

In the meantime, we are living in a period of *no dew and no rain* because the shepherds have not been faithful and because there is sin in the camp.

4
Sin in the Camp

Israel has sinned; they have violated my covenant, which I commanded them to keep. They have taken some of the devoted things; they have stolen, they have lied, they have put them with their own possessions. That is why the Israelites cannot stand against their enemies; they turn their backs and run because they have been made liable to destruction. I will not be with you anymore unless you destroy whatever among you is devoted to destruction.

Joshua 7:11,12

One of the purposes of this book is to try to explain scripturally, prophetically, and apostolically what has been happening in the Body of Christ over the past several years and what we can look forward to in the future. Another way of describing what is happening is to realize how God handles things when there is *sin in the camp*, because there definitely is sin in our camp.

In the book of Joshua, Israel had an astounding victory at Jericho — but then followed a significant defeat. Why? The reason revealed by God (Joshua 7) was *sin in the camp*. One man, Achan, had disobeyed God by stealing and hiding that which was to have been devoted to God. His sin was similar to that of Ananias and Sapphira who lied concerning their offering to God. (Acts 5:1-10.)

51

The sin that is in our camp today is similar to that of Achan, Ananias, and Sapphira: covetousness, greed, and idolatry. Those things are *gross violations of our covenant relationship* with God, and they have caused God's glory to depart until we repent.

Where Did We Go Wrong?

> **"Why did the Lord bring defeat upon us today before the Philistines? Let us bring the ark of the Lord's covenant from Shiloh, so that it may go with us and save us from the hand of our enemies."**
>
> **1 Samuel 4:3**

All through Israel's history, there were instances of God's glory departing because of sin in the camp, or because of wrongdoing by sheep and shepherds. Years after Joshua's day and years before Ezekiel's day, we can see another example of this. In First Samuel 4:3, a heart-rending question was asked of God by some terribly disillusioned Israelites. And today, disillusioned Christians are asking the same questions:

Why has disaster befallen us today?

Why have so many churches split?

Why have so many ministries dissolved?

Why have so many Christians fallen away from God in such deplorable and unrelenting defeat?

Accompanying God's judging of the sheep and the shepherds is the resulting loss of His glory, or the anointing of God's special power among His people.

Israel fought hard in her battle with the Philistines, but in the process she lost the Ark of the

Covenant, the place of God's anointing. There was nothing wrong with fighting her enemies, but there *is* a wrong way to handle the anointing.

The Church has fought valiant battles with the enemy of secular humanism, but in the process, we have forgotten how to handle the "Ark of the Lord." Consequently, we have lost the anointing that brings God's power into manifestation, although we have the largest churches, ministries, and budgets in the history of Christianity. There are certain ways God prescribed in the Bible to handle His glory.

The Ark represented God's presence, power, and protection. It was the physical and visible energy of God in and upon Israel. The Ark was the testimony of God among His people and the place where His Shekinah, His glory, rested among Israel.

We do not have a physical Ark today, but we have the spiritual Ark of the Covenant in the heart of each born again person. We have the presence of God in His people and in His Church. God testifies to and of Himself in the heart of the believer in the presence of a hostile and doubting world.

The glory of the Lord departed from Israel when they lost the Ark of the Covenant while in battle with the Philistines. (1 Sam. 4-7.) Did you know that you can lose the anointing right in the middle of your struggle against the enemy?

There is a small measure of the anointing in many churches, but we do not really feel, sense, or see that special and powerful presence of God in a conspicuous way. We see the works of the flesh and the works of man. We see numbers, conferences, seminars, schools, praise and worship, instruments and choirs. But where is that special anointing that breaks the yoke of bondage and delivers people from sin, sickness, and death?

When I was growing up, the word *salvation* meant not only being born again but being delivered from sin on a daily basis. Salvation was not just deliverance from a future hell. Being born again meant deliverance from present sinfulness — the habits, hungers, and hobbies of our carnal nature. Today, however, many people say, "I'm saved," and do anything they want to do, live any way they want to live, commit any sin they want to commit, while all the time claiming to be "the righteousness of God!" What a travesty of God's Word!

Everyone wants the power of God to manifest. We all want people to get up out of wheelchairs and walk. We want the power of God to be manifested all over the place. But that kind of thing only happens in an atmosphere of humility, holiness, and obedience that brings God's presence and favor upon us.

The reason these things are not happening today is because most of us cannot stand the spiritual atmosphere that His presence demands. Just as Ananias and Sapphira could not practice falsehood while in His presence and live, we too must abandon our flesh and sanctify ourselves in order to stand in or live through such a powerful presence of God.

There will be no Pentecost before purity. If the glory of God were to fall in most churches as it fell in New Testament apostolic times, most of the people would drop dead as did Ananias and his wife. Too much flesh, too much carnality, and too much human manipulation are going on in God's Church.

I Did It My Way

The first hint of the answer to why all these things have happened to us is found in the last half of First Samuel 4:3:

> **Let us bring the ark of the Lord's covenant from Shiloh, so that it** (some translations say "He") **may go with us and save** (rescue) **us from the hand of our enemies.**

The Israelites had undertaken a battle against the Philistines without the accompaniment of the Ark — which means, they had fought in the flesh and in their own power. As a result, they suffered a miserable defeat. The priesthood under Eli had become quite degenerate, and so had the spiritual state of the nation in general. Eli, although personally a good man, was a weak and indecisive leader and a weak and permissive father. Because of his irresponsible leadership, he was replaced by Samuel who represented a fresh generation of priestly and prophetic judgment on Israel and the initiation of a new era.

The word *prophet* occurs only occasionally before Samuel, such as in Genesis 20:7 and Exodus 7:1, but Samuel, it seems, was the official founder of a regular order of prophets and founder of the prophetic ministry in Israel. A similar occurrence is taking place in the Body of Christ today. A priestly and prophetic judgment is coming upon the Church of the 20th century. It will replace the "old guard" and usher in the 21st century move of the Holy Spirit.

Another word for *judgment* is "verdict." A *verdict* is a decision resulting from an investigation. *Judgment* is action taken based on the results of an inquiry or a test. Remember the handwriting on the wall in Daniel 5:25-28? Verse 27 says, **You have been weighed on the scales and found wanting ....** Such is the case in God's Church today. God's response is as it was in Daniel's day and in Samuel's day — removal of the old leaders and anointing of a new leadership. His response is *a changing of the guard.*

Familiarity Breeds Contempt

Israel had become so familiar with success when they were accompanied by the Ark that they grew careless and cocky and lost their reverence and consecration to God. Going into battle without the Ark or pursuing a noble cause without God's assistance will never work. God will not bless works of the flesh! Regardless of how well-intentioned the person, minister, or ministry is, if the effort is not anointed of God, it is an exercise in futility, and failure is inevitable.

In the past eight or ten years, I have talked with dozens of ministers — young and old, male and female — who started out in positive Holy Spirit zeal. They flowed in God's precious anointing which came as a result of prayer, fasting, and reverent consecration to God. That initial consecration brought them much success in every way. The money began to flow in. Name and face recognition made them popular, both in their local churches and across the nation. Their ministries became greatly in demand.

However, along with success came over-whelming busyness. Prayer, study of the Word, and fellowship with the Lord gradually became replaced by business: traveling, building projects, counseling, fellowshipping, and so forth. But success rolled on unimpeded. And that is where the danger lies. The anointing never comes abruptly upon a person's life and ministry, and it never leaves abruptly.

The Holy Spirit slowly and gradually covers your life, as you give up area after area. You may pray and fast, weep and work, and seek the face of God for years. Then one day you finally realize the anointing is there. The Holy Spirit is all over you, and everything you do is blessed.

I am learning that success is not a destination, it is a journey. It is not a coronation but a process. Anointed ministry is like money — it is not what you make that counts, but what you keep. Only on our knees can we really hear from God and attain both direction and discipline in accomplishing all our goals, fulfilling all our dreams and fighting all our battles. We must take His anointing with us into every situation in our lives.

Keepers of the Ark: Corruption

After Israel realized they had not been fighting with the Ark present, they sent back for it.

> **So the people sent men to Shiloh, and they brought back the ark of the covenant of the Lord Almighty, who is enthroned between the cherubim. And Eli's two sons, Hophni and Phineas, were with the ark of the covenant of God.**
> **1 Samuel 4:4**

As we read on in this chapter, we find that they lost the battle again and suffered "extremely heavy losses" even with the Ark present. How can you have the Ark of God present, have talents and operate in the calling of God, and still lose battles and live in defeat? How could a man like Jimmy Swaggart, who ministered under the anointing of God, fail so miserably and have been living in such moral defeat?

Look at Eli's sons, who were with the Ark of God. They were the official "keepers of the Ark." That means they were the "caretakers and guardians" of Israel's anointing. They were the sons of the High Priest of Israel, which made them also priests. They were not only of the tribe of Levi but direct descendants of Aaron. Both of them had been called and ordained of God to function in the priestly offices. Notice what Scripture says of the characters of these priests. They were guilty of both moral and ethical improprieties, but what offended the Lord most was the stunning and staggering indictment in First Samuel 2:17:

> This sin of the young men was very great in the Lord's sight, for they were treating the Lord's offering with contempt.

How typical a sin. God was not pleased with the way they were handling the offerings. Does that sound familiar? Haven't we heard that before, especially recently?

Offerings Are Part of Worship

Adultery, fornication, and other sexual sins are sins of the flesh. However, mishandling the Lord's offerings is a sin against the Spirit of God. Offerings given and received are a sacred act of worship. The offering is just as sacred as prayer, praise, or communion. It is as sacred an act of worship as Scripture reading or even preaching.

I pray the day will return when benevolent and charitable giving will not be seen as merely fund raising for some building project or some philanthropic gesture of religious piety. I pray for the day when giving to God will be regarded as a spiritual, reverent, and joyful act of obedience and an expression of our love and faith in a Holy God. Until that happens, regardless of how much money is raised or spent, God will not honor it with His blessing or His favor. The project may look good and be very well-intentioned, but God will not establish covenant with it.

The Church today needs to get rid of the sin in the camp and learn all over again how to handle the anointing.

5

As for You, My Flock

"'As for you, my flock, this is what the Sovereign Lord says: *I will judge between* one sheep and another, and between *rams and goats* (v. 17). Is it not enough for you to feed on the good pasture? *Must you also trample the rest of the pasture with your feet?* (v. 18). Is it not enough for you to drink clear water? *Must you also muddy the rest with your feet? Must my flock feed on what you have trampled and drink what you have muddied with your feet?* (v. 19).

"'Therefore this is what the Sovereign Lord says to them: See, I myself will judge between the fat sheep and the lean sheep (v. 20). Because you shove with flank and shoulder, butting all the weak sheep with your horns until you have driven them away, I will save my flock, and they will no longer be plundered. I will judge between one sheep and another (vv. 21,22).

Ezekiel 34:17-22

In the Bible, sheep (a ram is a male sheep) received by far more attention than any other animal. They played an important role in the domestic, civic, and religious life of the Israelites. The earliest mention of sheep is in Genesis 4:2 (KJV) where it is said that **Abel was a keeper of sheep.**

Both Hebrew and Arab shepherds had to move to new locations whenever pasturage ran out. This led to a nomadic, or wandering, existence and to the use of tents as houses. Water requirements meant that the shepherd had to know where the streams and wells could be found, and his movements with the flock were governed accordingly.

The more the rains, the greener the pasture, and the less travel was necessary. The larger the flock, the more trouble it was to move them. So *the good shepherd learned to pray for rain.*

In Ezekiel's time, God noticed among the Israelites a bad spirit of greed, carelessness, and what we call today "sloppy *agape*." It was not that the sheep were not being fed. In fact, they apparently were eating more than their fair share. They had eaten up all the good pasture. (v. 18.)

Today, in some circles, all you hear is "the Word, the Word, the Word — got to have more of the Word." We have received the Word, but instead of growing spiritually, many of us have just grown fat. I call it "inflated truth." There is nothing wrong with the meat itself, but it is surrounded by too much fat. We sheep, particularly Full Gospel sheep, have become fat.

I used to watch my late grandmother, whom we called "Big Mama," clean and prepare chicken for dinner. Before she ever fried the chicken, she would hold it under the faucet with the water running hard and fast. While she was washing the chicken, she would pick as much fat off each piece as she possibly could. She would pick it off with her fingers, and then scrape it with a knife until she was satisfied.

Countless times, I have heard her say, "I don't like no fat on my chicken."

Hophni and Phinehas, the corrupt sons of Eli, were guilty of going *after* the fat. So are many of today's Church leaders.

> Why do you honor your sons more than me by *fattening* yourselves on the choice parts of every offering ... ?
>
> 1 Samuel 2:29

Coveteousness and greed is a form of idolatry. Yes, there is a greed for the Word that counterfeits hunger for the Word and becomes idolatry. Hunger comes from the spirit of man, but greed from the soul (mind and emotions). I am not sure how it happened, but some people actually have fallen into the error of worshipping the written Word, quoting it almost as some form of hex or voodoo incantation.

That spirit is not of the Lord. It is the same erroneous spirit Satan used in tempting Jesus as He came out of His wilderness fast. It is a spirit of excess that shows up not only at the dining room table, but it is reflected in the grandiose plans, projects, and programs of many ministries today. Because of yielding to this spirit of "gluttony," or spirit of excess, these ministries always seem to be in the middle of some great financial crisis.

Muddying the Water for Others

As a result of our "obese" souls, God is accusing His Church today of trampling the "leftovers" underfoot. (v. 18.) That means many of us have left the footprints of our ungodly walk in the pastures for other less fortunate and weaker sheep to try to eat around. The pushy, abrasive, and arrogant attitudes of some sheep are indicative of lack of holy exercise.

We are standing on the promises, but sitting on the premises, and our walk is heavy and sluggish. We are leaving sloppy tracks behind us that are ugly in the sight of the Lord.

The same principle is involved when it comes to drinking water. As I said earlier, water in Scripture is often used metaphorically of the Holy Spirit. God's indictments against His sheep in Israel — and I believe also against His sheep today — have to do with *feet*, or with attitudes and behavior (soul problems), not with the heart.

The Israelites of Ezekiel's day apparently had good hearts, but their walk was bad. They ate the best pasture (Word) and drank the best water (Spirit), *but the food and drink were not being allowed to affect their walk with God or their conduct toward their fellow sheep.*

The unholy lifestyle of a carnal Christian who attends a Spirit-filled church where plenty of the anointed Word is preached is a very confusing thing. An unholy walk — regardless of how deep, cool, pure, plenteous, or refreshing the water is — will cause murkiness, mud, and sludge in the water. Then that mud will be stirred up by overfed, overweight, and underdone Christians whose **god is their stomach** (Phil. 3:19) — (their minds or their emotions).

The primary standard or principle of Christ is *love.* Jesus said:

> **By this shall all men know that ye are my disciples, if ye have love one to another.**
> **John 13:35 KJV**

A truly spiritual Christian will not push, shove, and poke at others, especially the weak, the way rams bully the ewes and lambs. Proud and arrogant Christians have driven many poor souls away from the water (Holy Spirit) and straight into the hands of the devil. The Holy Spirit is grieved by that type of unholy lifestyle. And He denounced it in this 34th chapter of Ezekiel.

Jesus addressed this in different words in Matthew 18:6:

> **If anyone causes one of these little ones who believe in me to sin** (stumble or fall away) **it would be better for him to have a large millstone hung around his neck and to be drowned in the depths of the sea.**

Also in Matthew, Jesus is quoted as saying, **Inasmuch as ye have done it unto one of the *least of these my brethren*, ye have done it unto me** (Matt. 25:40 KJV). If we could ever realize that we will be judged on our dealings with our brothers and sisters in the Body *as if we were dealing directly with Jesus*, we would immediately change our ways and attitudes. God wants us to love each other the way He loves us. When we do, we will see the showers of blessing.

Judging Between Rams and Goats

In verses 17-20, God said He would judge the sheep three ways:

1. General judgment — between one sheep and another. (Judgment of how we treat our brothers and sisters in the Lord.)

2. Judgment of our spirits — between rams and goats. (A goat is someone who really is not born again.)

3. Judgment of our souls — between the fat and the lean. (Judgment as to whether we have sought the Word for mental knowledge or emotional satisfaction, rather than for spiritual growth which *will* show up in changes in our lives.)

We have already dealt with the analogy between the first and third judgments of Israel in Ezekiel's day and God's judging within the Church today. So let's look at that second judgment, which was between rams and goats.

The difference between rams and goats seems obvious when judging them by their outward appearence, and it was really obvious in Ezekiel's day when most of the sheep were white and the goat herds of the Middle East were black. Many times, Palestinian shepherds had both sheep and goats in the same flock, but they do not graze well together. So at times it became necessary to separate them.[1]

At the time for separating the flocks, you would see the shepherd turning the sheep to the right and the goats to the left. Jesus used this custom in Matthew 25:32,33 to explain the separation of the nations at the endtime judgment. But what appears to be of special concern to God in this indictment against "His flock" is not based on outward appearances. In fact, the difference God sees actually has nothing whatsoever to do with externals.

Apparently, this is the same thing as separating the wheat from the tares, which I will talk about later

[1] Fred H. Wright, *Manners and Customs of Bible Lands* (Illinois: Chicago, The Moody Bible Institute of Chicago. Copyright © 1953, Moody Paperback Edition, 1983), pp. 166, 167.

in this book. There comes a time in the affairs of God's people when the goats have to be removed in order to protect the food and growth of the sheep.

A Covenant of Cleansing

Verse 25 of Ezekiel 34 seems to suggest that the showers of blessing for which we are all waiting will follow directly behind a *covenant* God promises to make with His people Israel.

> "'I will make a covenant of peace with them and rid the land of wild beasts so that they may live in the desert and sleep in the forests in safety.'"

The *covenant* is God's promise to bring peace by cleansing the land of wild beasts *after His people humble themselves and turn from their wicked ways.* The term *wild beasts* is used in the Bible many times as a figure of speech for "wild, false or erroneous doctrines" (teachings or teachers). False prophets, teachers with false doctrines, cults, gurus, and mystics have invaded the religious world in general and their heinous results have caused both spiritual and psychological havoc on the people.

This has been possible because of unspiritual and irresponsible leadership in the Church. God denounced that kind of leadership:

> Therefore, you shepherds, hear the word of the Lord: As surely as I live, declares the Sovereign Lord, because my flock lacks a shepherd and so has been plundered and has become food for all the wild animals, and because my shepherds did not search for my flock but cared for themselves rather than for my flock, therefore, O shepherds, hear the word of the Lord:

> This is what the Sovereign Lord says: I am against the shepherds and will hold them accountable for my flock. I will remove them from tending the flock so that the shepherds can no longer feed themselves. I will rescue my flock from their mouths, and it will no longer be food for them.
>
> **Ezekiel 34:7-10**

The state of the Church leadership today has allowed the sheep to be plundered. But God is in the process of "rescuing" His sheep from the hands of unfaithful shepherds.

Also, every Christian goes through wilderness areas in his life, through fiery trials or through thick and congested forests of underbrush where the shadows and dampness of loneliness and fear are all around. Usually during those times, the beasts appear with their lies and seducing spirits. The deserts and thick forests of self-pity are where those spirits live, lurk, and breed their heinous offspring.

When people are going through tests or trials and become despondent and in despair, they are especially vulnerable at that time to the erroneous teachings of a sometimes well-meaning but misguided so-called teacher or sometimes a layperson. Either way, if the blind lead the blind, both fall into the ditch. (Matt. 15:14.)

In the cleansing covenant, God does not promise to remove all deserts and forests; He simply promises a safe passage through them.

Cleansing Is Followed by Blessings

The cleansing process, God says, will be followed by blessings, and the blessings come in showers. The corrective measures taken by God in

Ezekiel 34 in dealing both with shepherds and sheep are not punishments but rather show His love for them and His desire to bless them.

God was aware of the fact that both the land and the people were impoverished. (vv. 27,29.) Verse 29 particularly seems to indicate the presence of famine in the land:

> I will provide them a land renowned for its crops, and they will no longer be victims of famine in the land ... .

The blessings God spoke of are material as well as spiritual. The land evidently was being wasted away, and lack of rain had caused severe drought. The second part of verse 26 is **I will send down showers in season**, then the Lord added, **there will be showers of blessing** (material wealth). Sometimes God sends only spiritual rain and spiritual blessings. Other times He sends natural rain with natural, or material, blessings. I have learned to enjoy and appreciate both.

With the "beasts" and the "bullies" gone, or at least in check, the blessings are then showered upon us to refresh, restore and revive.

But there are conditions to God's covenants with man, and the conditions on our side are simple: to hear and obey.

Isaiah 1:19,20 says:

> If you are willing and obedient, you will eat the best from the land; but if you resist and rebel, you will be devoured by the sword.

Willing obedience brings you the best of the land. Rebelling causes you to be devoured by the sword, or whatever the "sword" represents in your life. Let's remove the sin out of our lives and out of our churches, and get ready for a great move of God.

6
I Hear God Walking

In the middle of the horrible tragedies that have taken place in the Body of Christ over the past year and a half, I can hear God walking. My ears are like Elijah's: *I hear the sound of the abundance of rain.* In the midst of everything the Body of Christ is facing, I hear the sound of God walking in the garden, and His footsteps sound like glory to me.

I do not want to run and hide behind the trees. For regardless of how thick the trunk of the tree was in the Garden of Eden or how deep its roots dug into the ground, it began to tremble when God walked by. Every bird began to sing. Today, as many of the Body sit hiding in sin, covering themselves with their own fig leaves, I hear the sound of the walking of God. I hear a soft, gentle breeze blowing through the trees.

Can you hear the sound of the footsteps of God walking through the garden of your despair? That is what God is doing now — walking through the gardens of our spirits — and I am encouraged in spite of all the bad news about the Church. Instead of running from God, I run directly into His presence. I do what Adam should have done, and the history of my life is changed. Yours can be changed in the same way — *if you understand what God really is saying.*

What Did God Really Say?

In order to put the problem of sin in the Body of Christ into perspective, we need to look all the way back to the beginning of mankind on earth. We need to look at the first sin.

The sin of Adam and Eve was the *first sin* in the entire history of man. It was not adultery or fornication. It was not theft or robbery. It was not murder. It was not even backbiting or gossip. Those sins and all other carnal, soulish, or spiritual sins followed in the wake — or were results of — the first sin.

All sin revolves around the fact that man does not really know what God said.

The devil knows God is real, but he challenges and attacks God's Word to man. Satan went to the woman first. He planted a wrong seed in Eve and out of that came the destruction of the world as God had created it. He did this by first questioning the word of God: "Did God *really* say? What did God *really* say?" (Gen. 3:1.)

Eve let the devil cause her to doubt what God had really said. As soon as he dropped that doubt in her mind, she began to get farther and farther off target. She began to focus on deception and misfocus on truth. That is what the devil does: He blinds and blurs your vision so that you cannot see truth. Then when you do not know truth, you cannot be free.

It is amazing how easily people can "eat of the forbidden fruit" and fall from truth into deception. A young lady I know who is married to a preacher "fell in love" with an associate in the church and began having a relationship with him. I have known the couple for years, but when she finally came to me, she already was saying things like:

"I love him. We have so much in common. We relate so well. He is a man of God, and when we talk, he ministers to me. It did not start out like this. I was lonely, and he was lonely, and we began to comfort one another. The Lord began to use him to help me. Now we both realize we made a mistake in our marriages, because we really were made for each other."

Deception. She has been blinded by the god of this world to where she cannot understand truth anymore. There was no way I could convince this young lady she had made a mistake. She was not willing to see the "bottom-line" truth: The young man with whom she was involved was another woman's husband, and she was another man's wife. So she believed a deception. Her natural feelings for the other man outweighed what God had said. Her desire for the fruit outweighed God's "Thou shall not eat."

Isn't it amazing that sin did not enter through adultery or lying, but through the mouth? One piece of fruit threw everything out of kilter with God. Sin in the form of the fruit of the tree of knowledge of good and evil still looks good for food. It still looks pleasing to the eye and desirable for gaining wisdom. And Eve took some, ate it, and gave it to her husband.

I do not know what Adam was doing, but the way the Word is written, he was there along with her. Did he watch her sin? Did he know what she was doing? Did she consult him about it?

Perhaps she was like an old girlfriend of my grandfather's, who said to my sister once, "Honey, don't go out and do things on your own. You must always insult your husband on things like this."

She meant *consult,* but she said *insult.* Some ladies get the two words mixed up. They always insult their husbands, not consult them, before they do things. Eve apparently neither insulted nor consulted. She just went on and did her own thing, then when she got through doing it, she turned around and involved him in her sin.

Notice that God had a stronger influence on Adam than He did on Eve; Satan had a stronger influence on Eve than he had on Adam, but Eve had a stronger influence on Adam than either God or Satan. The devil apparently could not get directly at Adam, so he came indirectly.

Satan could not interrupt the vertical relationship between Adam and God, so he used the horizontal relationship between Adam and Eve to disrupt the vertical relationship. Adam had a beautiful relationship with God. They walked and talked together. So if Satan cannot break your relationship with God, he will try to break your relationship with man which will affect your relationship with God.

How God Deals With Crisis

What happened when God caught up with Adam and Eve in the evening? He had a crisis to deal with. What did He do? He blocked the tree of life. Do you realize that Adam and Eve had no idea what *death* was? Nothing had ever died, not a plant, an animal, or a human being. God said, in essence:

"Never let them eat from it, because they have become like us. If they eat of the tree of life, they will live eternally in this fallen state as demons do. A demon cannot be redeemed. Don't let them eat from the tree, so that they can be saved from this curse of eternal separation from Me."

Then he jumped several thousand years and got another tree ready. He called it "Calvary." About this second tree, God said:

"Let mankind eat of this tree of life, and I will give Jesus a love for the human race like Adam had for Eve, a love so intense that while they are yet sinners, He Who knows no sin will become sin and identify with them. He will suffer the consequences of sin so they may be redeemed. He will love man more than Himself, enough to give up all of the glories of heaven and His divine status to live on earth in a fallen state with mankind. It will be the same kind of thing Adam did for Eve, only this time it will *restore* the tree of life to man. It will mean life and not death."

> **For the wages of sin is death, but the gift of God is eternal life in Christ Jesus our Lord.**
> **Romans 6:23**

What if Adam had run up to God instead of hiding when God called?

Suppose Adam had said, "I wondered if You would come back. I have sinned."

If Adam had been sorry and repented and called out to God in tears for forgiveness, I believe the history of the world would have been different.

David repented in tears, sackcloth, and ashes for his sin with Bathsheba and for his murder of her husband. Their first child died, but God's forgiveness was so complete that Bathsheba was able to remain David's wife, and their next son lived. He was named Solomon.

Why did God put the tree of knowledge of good and evil in the Garden of Eden in the first place? God made man in His likeness and image. That means He made him a moral being. In order to be moral, you have to have a choice. There is no such thing as morality without a choice. God did not make mankind to be puppets. He made us able to make choices. However, when Adam and Eve made the wrong choice and elevated mind over spirit, mankind got off balance.

The Body Has Fallen to Three Weaknesses

What is happening in the Body of Christ worldwide, but particularly in this nation, is that it has fallen prey to three human weaknesses, the same three that caused Eve to fall out of fellowship with God:

The lust of the flesh, the lust of the eyes, and the pride of life. (1 John 2:16 KJV.)

Eve saw that the fruit of the tree was good for food [lust of the flesh], pleasing to the eye [lust of the eye], and desirable for gaining wisdom [pride of life]. Today, we all still face those three tendencies. It is almost impossible, without the supernatural power of the Holy Spirit, to see something that embodies one or more of those temptations and not touch it.

Also, what Adam and Eve did when they had fallen into these temptations is what we still do: We "sew fig leaves together" and make coverings for ourselves. Our coverings are religious ritualism designed to cover our own nakedness, our own faults, without going through the true atonement, the blood of Jesus.

But right in the midst of their failure, God came to Adam and Eve. The Lord is so wonderful. He does not reject us when we break fellowship, but He comes to us. Sometimes we ignore the walking of God in the Garden and try to maintain our own covering, calling it "holiness" when it is only our fig leaves — the traditions and doctrines (works) of man.

Relationship, Repentance, and Renewal

Not too long ago, I had a problem with my back. If your back is out of whack, everything else hurts! As I was in pain at every little move, the Spirit of God began to deal with me about the pain in the Body of Christ. There seems to be a lot of pain because the very spinal cord of the Church has been injured. Every nerve is sensitive, and the slightest movement causes pain.

The Holy Spirit spoke to me and said, "You cannot teach forgiveness before you teach repentance. I have heard the most eloquent messages on forgiveness and on grace and on God covering man's sins with the blood, but I have to sit on the sidelines until there is repentance."

I feel the Spirit of God is about to move on the face of the deep, and when He does, you have never heard preachers preach as they will then. Today, we are teaching the best and giving the best instructions about faith, healing, deliverance, and baptism in the Holy Spirit that has been taught since the days of the early Church, but the Spirit of God is waiting on the sidelines.

Relationship leads to repentance, and repentance always leads to restoration and renewal.

The problem of sin is that it is darkness and obscures truth. But the hope is that we can go back and rewrite the scroll. (Jer. 36:28. See "Take Another Scroll," Chapter 14.) God rewrote His scroll when the devil "burned" access to the first tree through Adam and Eve. God's rewriting was victorious in Jesus.

Light Also Involves Sight

Another way to look at this is to consider the word *light*. Some definitions include "illumination, revelation, truth, awareness, sight." When God said, **Let there be light** (Gen. 1:3), He also was saying, "Let there be *sight*." Light helps you. If it is dark, you cannot see the target, the mark. There is no darkness in God, the Word says. (1 John 1:5.) Sin is darkness. If there is darkness in your relationship, you focus on it and miss the light. The world cannot see the light. The world cannot see the goal of God. Having grown up in the darkness of the world, even as Christians we have spent our lives aiming at — but missing — the mark. We are out of focus, and that is the devil's intent: to blind the eyes, the vision, the sight.

The Word says that **In the beginning God created the heavens and the earth** (Gen. 1:1). The next verse says that darkness was over the surface of the deep, and then the Spirit of God hovered or moved over the waters. In other words, the Spirit of God created the atmosphere for the speaking of the Word of God. No matter how much or how well a person speaks, if the atmosphere is not charged by the Spirit of God to make it receptive to the Word of God, his words are ineffective.

Before God ever said anything, the Spirit of God moved upon the face of the deep. *Then* God spoke, and when He spoke, the first thing He said was, **Let there be light** (sight, illumination, revelation, truth).

God began the earth on *truth*. He began His move with light, illumination, and awareness. And He called the light *day* and the darkness *night*. (Gen. 1:5.)

God's first act after speaking forth light was to separate light from dark. He separated natural light from natural darkness and since the fall of Adam and Eve, He has been separating spiritual light from spiritual darkness: day from night, and righteousness from sin.

Once the well-known Christian singer Carman and I went into a bar in Hawaii because the Holy Spirit had led him to find a certain young woman and minister to her. I was so embarrassed! I did not want to go into that place.

I said, "Somebody is going to see me," and the Lord answered, "That's what I want."

But I thought it would be one of my church members or someone who had seen me on television. I thought someone would see us and go tell other people: "I saw Brother Carlton Pearson in a bar!"

We walked in, and everyone stopped what they were doing and looked at us — two evangelists walking into a hole-in-the-wall bar.

I was still mumbling about "somebody will see us," when the Holy Spirit said, "You are the light of the world." I heard Him, but it did not really register.

We walked over to some chairs — and it seemed everyone's eyes followed us — and as we sat down, the Holy Spirit again said, "You are the light of the world."

This time, I answered, "What do you mean?"

He said, "It was dark in this bar until you two came in. They were in darkness, but you brought light."

As a Christian, you have the power of God and the light of God within you. You can go anywhere, through the den of lions, through the burning fiery furnaces of life *if the Lord sends you.*

If you go on your own, you may be into presumption, not faith. But if God sends you, do not be afraid to go anywhere to minister. We won two of the people in that bar to Christ that night.

God is speaking to us today sort of like a wife might her husband, "I don't want another fur. I don't want another diamond. I don't want a bigger house or car. I want *you.*"

Or it is like a man might say to his wife, "Sweetheart, it is not the meals you cook or the clothes you clean. It's not even the way you take care of the children, but I want you to touch me, sit with me, and talk to me. Let's pray together. Let's really get to know one another."

We need to allow the Holy Spirit to convict us of our sins, but we do not need to allow the devil to tempt us into condemnation of others or of ourselves.

David cried out to God:

> **For I know my transgressions, and my sin is always before me.**
>
> **Psalm 51:3**

One of my board members told me, "Brother Carlton, whatever happens, no matter how blessed you are by God, stay humble. Don't let your head get big. Stay before God."

I said, "Yes, Sir! I have a built-in machine. I know my transgressions. My imperfections, human weaknesses, and frailties are ever before me. I won't ignore them."

I live in the light of conviction, *not in the darkness of condemnation.* I do not walk in condemnation, but I live under conviction almost constantly. I will not ignore the conviction. The Word is like walking by a mirror. Few people can resist at least checking their appearance in a mirror when they pass it. The Word is light in a world of darkness. The Word is like one of those makeup mirrors women use to highlight their faces while they put on makeup. If you really look into the mirror of the Word, you can see yourself better.

Looking into the mirror of the Word also shows up the delusions of Satan, which are increasing and being magnified by the world.

Satan's Tactics of Destruction

Some Christians are eating because of stress. They cannot control their appetites. When they gain weight, it fuels self-hate. They look at themselves in the mirror and feel so ugly, fat, heavy, and miserable. Some Christians are oppressed by spiritual bulimia or anorexia nervosa. These lying delusions of Satan to destroy men and women are in the church, not just the world!

Not long ago, a preacher rushed up to me, the first time we ever met. He took me by the hand and asked if he could talk to me. This is a pastor with more than a thousand attending his church. I had met his wife, a beautiful lady, the night before. He did not know me, but he had heard of me.

He said, "Man, I cannot handle the women in my church!"

I asked, "Wasn't that your wife I met the other night? She's lovely. Don't you love her?"

He said, "Yes, I do, but I cannot handle these women. They are coming out of the woodwork, and I have lost my control."

So I shared with him what the Holy Spirit had told me.

I said, "The Spirit of God has shown me that a horde of demons has been unleashed from the pits of hell — sex demons aimed at men of God."

The Lord showed me demons flying out like bats and attaching themselves to ministries, to staff members of ministries, to leaders in the Church, and these men are shocked. They do not know what has happened to them. I am angry at the demons, and I am angry at the apathy and lethargy which we display in the Church and to which so many have fallen prey. We need to recognize the enemy.

Evil spirits of pride, ego, or lust come to us and say, "Just leave us alone. Leave us in here. We will never embarrass you. We will never tell anyone we are here. We won't interrupt your life or your ministry. We won't interrupt your marriage, but we have to stay somewhere. Don't kick us out. Don't cast us out."

Their voices say, "Don't identify us. Don't go to a church where they will recognize us."

But the Holy Spirit said to me, "Those things which have been in darkness, which have been hidden, are going to be uncovered. Warn the people. Tell them to get ready. Tell them their whole confidence has got to be in Me, because of what I am going to reveal. I am going to heal them. I am going to pull them through, but *you warn the people there is a shaking coming that will shake the earth to its very foundation.*"

The shaking has already begun.

Men Will See the Awe-fulness of God

The miracles and signs that many are looking for in this new move of the Spirit are not going to be the kinds of things they are anticipating. The miracles and signs we are going to see may not only be cancers disappearing, blind eyes popping open, or deaf ears hearing. There *will* be those kinds of things, but these are the kinds of wonders we are going to see:

A man or woman of God will walk into a room and be called on to speak like a two-edged sword. It may be in the market place. It may be on Wall Street.

It may be up in the viewing galleries of the Senate or the House of Representatives. The Spirit of God may come upon a Supreme Court justice supernaturally. If He can speak through a donkey as He did to Balaam, He can talk through some of those politicians!

Suddenly, a Supreme Court justice may rise up and say exactly what God wants him to say — as a sign. Or there may be a time when the Spirit of God will come into a place, and an obedient and anointed believer will walk through there and speak the will of God. If the people there laugh and jeer at them, that whole building may fall down on them, and every one of those who jeered would be picked up dead.

Two or three people may be in a room somewhere lying on their faces before God, and the whole house will look as if it is on fire. Someone will call the fire department, but when they arrive, they will only find a few people on their faces before God. The things that God is going to do next are going to be things to cause men to see His awe-fulness. They will be awe-inspiring wonders, things that will bring us to our knees.

Scientists are going to have to say, "We cannot explain this. We do not want to say it is God, but we cannot explain it. This is a very strange occurrence. People saw the building on fire — but it wasn't. They saw people go into it, but when firemen got in there, no one was there. And we do not know where they went!"

I believe people are going to walk with God like Enoch and suddenly disappear. I believe it is going to happen in Hollywood and in Washington. It is going to happen in Tulsa, and it may not be the people whom you would think.

> **Create in me a pure heart, O God, and renew a steadfast spirit within me.**
>
> **Psalm 51:10**

There is a cleansing and a purging coming. Will you be in that number? Will you let God clean you up? I want there to be repentance. My heart is broken for God's people.

7

Test the Spirits:

Deception Walks the Earth

> Dear friends, do not believe every spirit, but test the spirits to see whether they are from God, because many false prophets have gone out into the world. This is how you can recognize the Spirit of God: Every spirit that acknowledges that Jesus Christ has come in the flesh is from God, but every spirit that does not acknowledge Jesus is not from God. This is the spirit of the antichrist, which you have heard is coming and even now is already in the world.
>
> **1 John 4:1-3**

We have already established that God is doing the shaking in the Church today. But Satan is taking advantage of the shaking to move his own devices, schemes, and systems forward. Christians need to learn to test the spirits at work in order to know when to resist and when not to mourn but go on with God's work.

To *stand in these critical days* requires wisdom and understanding as well as courage.

There is a crafty spirit at work among God's people, a spirit of deception, a subtle lying spirit that is so convincing in itself that many people fall for it. We need to remember that rat poison is 90 percent good corn. Only the 10 percent strychnine makes it lethal.

The devil seldom tells a complete untruth. He always has enough truth to disguise the lie, so that you are caught up in the *fact* of what he said rather than the *truth* of what he meant.

A young girl in my church, Mari Clere, writes poems. The Sunday morning that I preached on this, she handed me a poem written five days earlier.

In the Devil's Mind

He's God's property,
   the label says he's bought.
But I'll ease into his mind
   and get control of his thoughts.
I'll take his heart and make it cold.
Then to me he will be sold.

I'll make him think it's all a game.
And fill his life with doubt and pain.
I'll tear his life all apart.
Then leave him dying of an empty heart.

I love to deceive, it's what I do best.
By putting these Christians to a worldly test,
I get their attention, and lead them on,
I make them think nothing is wrong.

Then I drag them out through fire and rain,
Until their life is nothing but pain.
Then they blame God
   for not keeping them safe.

I leave them crying in a lonely place.
Until they see how badly they failed,
and then they'll join me here in hell.

This is my strategy: to do it my way.
I am a living deceiver both night and day.

The word *crafty* means "a misrepresentation of underlying objectives." The devil misrepresents his underlying objective. For instance, he said to Eve, **You will be like God, knowing good and evil** (Gen. 3:5b). That was a fact: after eating of the fruit, they were like God in one aspect — they had a knowledge of good and evil. But the underlying objective of the serpent was not to give them a truth to make them free, but a fact to bring them into death.

Innocence and Virtue Are Not Synonymous

God's underlying objective in telling them, "If you eat of that tree, you will surely die" (Gen. 2:17), was to keep them from dying. God's *fact* and His *truth* were the same, and His motive was to bring them into life. Adam and Eve were innocent, but not necessarily virtuous. Innocence is the state in which a child exists before he becomes accountable, before he knows the difference between right and wrong, good and evil. Virtue means coming face to face with temptation, knowing the difference, and *choosing* good while resisting evil.

We must learn how to resist the devil. We must become virtuous. The devil has come in our time with powerful delusions: the wiles of error and misrepresentation of truths of an essential nature. He has beguiled an entire generation into thinking that lust is love, that drugs and alcohol are a way to peace, and that greed is natural because material things are one of man's "rights."

He has taken good, perverted and distorted it, and made it into evil. The Bible says everything God made was good. If that is true, then what is evil? Evil is nothing more or less than a distortion or perversion of good.

Bait is only to allure you and to trap you. Fish who snap at the bait are deceived by the craftiness of the fisherman. A fish snaps at something dangling in the water that looks nutritious and attractive and looks like something the fish cannot live without — food. But it is a deception that will get him killed. The fish does not know what is on the other end of the line.

Christians must learn to check and see what is on the other end of the line from which the thing is dangling that looks so good. The devil has not reeled some Christians in yet, but he has them on the line. He is letting them run until they get tired, then he will reel them in. They will find the same habit, the same hunger that got them up against the boards the first time, pulling on them again. They are trying to resist, but they took the bait.

To keep from getting hooked by Satan, you must not take the bait. Once you take the bait — which is something you want or think you need — you are hooked.

Another way of looking at this would be an analogy to "playing by the rules." You may think you have won a race, but if you missed one of the rules, you can be disqualified at the finish line by a mere technicality.

Sin Often Camouflaged by Good Intentions

Satan plays down, or de-emphasizes, the ultimate consequences of your actions and disguises fact with "noble, or good, intentions." That is why the old adage says, "The road to Hell is paved with good intentions." Many Christians err while carrying out well-intentioned efforts. We do not do what God wanted us to do or do it when He wanted us to do it, but then we say, "Oh, well, God knows my heart is pure and that I meant well."

Christians easily excuse themselves from sloppy spiritual habits or even sinful habits by saying, "But that is really not in my heart. God knows my heart." Some of the errors Christians make are not necessarily moral but are ethical. However, sin is still sin regardless of its nature.

Have you ever had someone totally misunderstand what you said, or misinterpret your well-meaning intentions?

You say, "But I didn't mean it that way. I didn't want to hurt you. I'm sorry."

We are constantly doing that to God — always misinterpreting what He means. But He is changing all that. He is turning the whole Church around like a great ocean liner ponderously turning in the ocean. God is reminding us of His Deity. He is reminding us that He is in control.

He said, **Those who are led of the Spirit of God are sons of God** (Rom. 8:14).

We Must Understand the Spirit of Truth

The Church must get back to the point where we understand the Spirit of Truth, the Holy Spirit. I have never seen such a delusion on Christians, such a spirit of confusion, as I see today. Because of watching all the shameful things in the Church that are being published or aired through the media, people are absolutely confused. They cannot discern the will of God about anything: where to go to church, or even *if* they need to go at all, when to give, or to whom to give. Many have withdrawn from church altogether, and the enemy is confusing the issues in their thinking and making a playground of their minds.

The Bible says, **God is not a God of disorder, but of peace** (1 Cor. 14:33). He is not a god of confusion but of peace. The devil is the author of confusion. He is the spirit of lawlessness, the spirit of antichrist — antiorder, antistructure.

We have a lot of knowledge of the Word among the Christians in this country today. But as my associate pastor, Gary McIntosh, says, "Knowledge without revelation can bring destruction."

Wisdom is the ability to evaluate objectives with a view of their practical, or end, results. You have to be able to apply that knowledge through the guidance of the Holy Spirit. Wisdom comes through supernatural, divine understanding. The devil can quote Scriptures, so your testing of the spirits, or of the thoughts, actions, and attitudes that come to you, must be on the Word and on what the Holy Spirit witnesses in your heart.

We need to have a Spiritual automatic nervous system. The body has two systems, an involuntary (automatic) one and a voluntary one. If you itch, you *voluntarily* scratch, but if you get dust in your nose, you *involuntarily* sneeze. We need an involuntary and a voluntary devil-detection system.

If an evil spirit brings the idea of murder to most Christians, they involuntarily "sneeze" the thought out of their minds. They react automatically. But if the evil spirit brings a critical thought, it takes a voluntary act of resistance. The subtle thoughts and attitudes the deceiver brings as bait are the ones that hook us. First, we take the bait of the critical thought about the pastor. Then we begin to gossip and backbite, and finally, we move on to slander. We are hooked.

> **Be self-controlled and alert. Your enemy the devil prowls around like a roaring lion looking for someone to devour.**
>
> **1 Peter 5:8**

We need to recognize the sound of the deceiver roaring as a lion while he prowls up and down. We need to be alert and sober. When you hear that roar, acknowledge it. Don't try to ignore it by saying, "Well, praise God, I'll just pretend the devil's not here." No, just confront him head on. Say, "No!" The devil roars loud enough for you to be able to identify him, so there is no use going around saying, "I was deceived."

Victory in the next life depends on the gift of eternal life from Jesus; victory in this life depends on our walking in as much obedience (holiness) as possible through the Holy Spirit. We are not to walk around with a "holier-than-thou" attitude. We are to be humble, saying with the Apostle Paul:

"God, I struggle. I beat my body and bring under the flesh so that I will not be disqualified at the end of the line on a mere technicality. I want to run the race all the way and win." (1 Cor. 9:24-27.)

Weigh the Spirit Against the Word

All we have to do is weigh that spirit to make sure it is of God and that it agrees with the Word. If the Stock Market crashes, God is still God. If major ministries continue to go under, God is still God. Things are shaky, but Jesus is still Lord. Where He reigns, he pours. Let Him reign in you so He will rain on you.

God did not say to test the person. He said to test the spirit behind or in the person. Our enemy is Satan, not other people. But be on guard in your own life. Sometimes a wrong spirit may come and try to work through you, so you need to test your own motives and thoughts and behavior to see of what spirit they are — the Holy Spirit's or an evil spirit's.

The Apostle Paul said:

> So I find this law at work: When I want to do good, evil is right there with me. For in my inner being I delight in God's law; but I see another law at work in the members of my body, waging war against the law of my mind and making me a prisoner of the law of sin at work within my members. What a wretched man I am! Who will rescue me from this body of death? (Then he answered his own question.) Thanks be to God — through Jesus Christ our Lord!
>
> **Romans 7:21-25**

There are only three kinds of spirits that work in the world: The Holy Spirit, human spirits, and the unholy spirits of the devil.

You have a mind (soul), and you live in a body, but you *are* a spirit. It is up to you to decide how you are going to be influenced. Christians need to be able in these days to distinguish between the Holy Spirit, their own spirits, and evil spirits.

> **You, dear children, are from God and have overcome them, because the one who is in you is greater than the one who is in the world. They are from the world and therefore speak from the viewpoint of the world, and the world listens to them. We are from God, and whoever knows God listens to us; but whoever is not from God does not listen to us. This is how we recognize the Spirit of truth and the spirit of falsehood** (or the spirit of error).
>
> **1 John 4:4-6**

The Church must allow the Holy Spirit to be her guide and standard, because in the next four or five years, the need to judge between the Spirit of Truth and the spirit of error will be absolutely imperative. Thank God for His Holy Spirit.

8

Hidden Weapons of the Enemy

> Be self-controlled and alert. Your enemy the devil prowls around like a roaring lion looking for someone to devour. Resist him, standing firm in the faith, because you know that your brothers throughout the world are undergoing the same kind of sufferings.
>
> 1 Peter 5:8,9

One night early in 1988, I could not sleep — and I really needed to rest — but the Holy Spirit kept showing me things and dealing with me. The Lord showed me some hidden weapons of the enemy waiting for this hour. I saw some things that have not yet been leveled against the Church or its leadership — or they are just beginning to be unleashed against us.

What I saw was as if the Soviet Union had been coming up with different kinds of nuclear weaponry and other forms of warfare, such as germs and chemicals, of which the Western world was not aware. There *are* things in the arsenals of major world nations that are top secret. Whether they are indirect weapons — such as acid rain, or things that might affect weather conditions in other countries and cause disasters that look natural — or more conspicuous direct weapons, I am sure there are many things that would appall us if we knew of them.

Similarly, Satan has kept in reserve top-secret weaponry he plans to use against the Church in this hour. I saw in the spirit that there is going to be an increase of demonic warfare against the Church and its leadership. These attacks include increased emotional and psychological stress, unprecedented financial compromises, and attacks on families.

I saw ministers under so much financial pressure they were resorting to loan sharks. Organized crime has been made aware through recent media exposure of the fact that large sums of money are being handled in the Christian field. With teaching tapes, music, books and magazines, television programs, and so forth, billions of dollars are being handled in the Christian world each year. The crime world has never watched an industry succeed in this country that they did not try — and usually be successful at — getting their hands on some of the money.

Recently, we have heard of government leaders — actual heads of state — who were part of the drug traffic in their countries. Drug enforcement officers are being bought out by dealers. Organized crime has money, power, and influence; and I tell you, if Christians do not get to the place where the hand of God is protecting us, the devil will try to monopolize the very Church of Jesus Christ. And do not make the careless error of thinking he can not do it. He can do it — as long as he is dealing with a bunch of people who are not sensitive to the Holy Spirit, who are not willing to pay the price to live holy, and who are not praying and seeking the face of God.

The Spirit of God is grieved by what is happening today, because the healers are now sick.

The salt is losing its savor. (Matt. 5:13.) The things we are selling, we cannot buy.

The Weapon of Stress

In my spirit, I saw preachers under so much pressure that they would actually consult witches, palm readers, and fortune tellers, as Saul did when he lost his anointing. He consulted the Witch of Endor, who called up Samuel the prophet from his grave to speak to Saul. (1 Sam. 28:7-11.) Some theologians believe that was a demon. Others believe it actually was Samuel whom the Lord allowed to return to condemn or pass judgment on Saul. I do not know. But I do know there *is* such a thing as witchcraft and other forms of sorcery.

In fact, the word *music* comes from the word for "to muse," which means "to think." The word *amuse* actually means the opposite. It means "to stop thinking." The Greek word for *sorcery* is *pharmakia*, from which we get the English word *pharmacy* — drugs, chemicals, potions, and so forth.

We are living in a day full of sorcerers. The reason people take drugs is because they cannot face reality. Drugs make the mind listless and unresponsive. They deaden the senses to reality. When you go to the dentist, they give you an anesthetic. You are still hurting when they pull that tooth, but you do not know it. Once those nerves come back to life, they hurt. That is what happens when people take drugs to deaden reality or emotions. Once the drug wears off, the pain is still there and usually much worse.

Painkillers Are Dangerous Sometimes

Some time ago, I lifted weights in my home and pulled something in my back. At the time, I did not pay much attention to it. But three days later, I was playing tennis with my associate, Gary McIntosh, and I returned one of his serves — which came over the net like a nuclear weapon! As I reached out to swing and hit that ball, a pain hit me in the lower part of my back that nearly killed me. I let out a screech. At first, Gary thought I was rejoicing because I had returned his serve! He had to practically carry me off the court.

The doctor gave me something for pain, and I was still taking it on Sunday morning. I found it can be a dangerous thing to even take painkillers. Between the first and second service, my mind went blank. I lost all sense of who I was and what I was doing. I had to lean over to Gary and say, "What am I preaching this morning?" I had forgotten both my text and my subject.

The Holy Spirit said, "That is a sign in the natural of what is happening in the Church."

Men have lifted weights too heavy for themselves. Their building projects, television ministries, and fund-raising projects are all too heavy. They have wrenched their backs, torn their spines, even broken vertebrae. They are crippled, and the only way they can stand the pain is to drug themselves. In that delirious state, they are making other decisions that are plunging them farther into debt. A computer is not solving it, and a mailing list is not solving it.

Now the pressure has become so great, they do not know what to do. They are afraid someone is going to find out they are sick. They are afraid someone is going to find out they are in debt. I see this as a force of the devil coming against the Body of Christ. We cannot carry these things in the flesh any longer. The Holy Spirit is grieved.

God Is Not Through

My soul cried out as I wrestled with these things the night God showed them to me.

I said, "God, there has to be a way out. I am tired of even thinking about this kind of thing. I wanted 1988 to be a year of double-newness."

But things may get worse before they get better. Early in 1988, God had been speaking to me of this shaking, of dark clouds gathering. This one will bring the Church to her knees, He said. After that will come the mighty outpouring of the Holy Spirit. We must make sure our personal relationships with God are intact, that we have the intimacy and romance of God and the Holy Spirit, because we are not going to be able to depend on preachers, ministers, and organizations. Spiritual survival, if not natural survival, is going to depend on God and Him alone.

The Spirit of God spoke to my heart and said, "I am coming personally Myself with a winnowing fork in My hand. I am going to clean it up Myself, and I will tolerate nothing."

Much of the Church seems to be locked into pride, ego, and competition. We are not willing to rid ourselves of all that junk, and God says, "I am not going to tolerate it again." Some of us stop sinning for a little while, then we take the bait again, and go right back into the same sin. Most people have to watch constantly. God cannot relent for even a minute without them going back into the thing He just pulled them out of.

The night God gave me this prophetic warning, my heart kept saying, "God, have mercy. Have mercy. God, have mercy. Let this just be a dream, a nightmare. Don't let this be real. God, you are not really speaking to me. God, surely I am not really hearing this."

All the time, I kept hearing my own spirit say, **Have mercy on** ...(us), **O God, according to** *your* **unfailing love** (Ps. 51:1a).

There is this ray of hope: If we do not yield to the hidden weapons and attacks of Satan, we will not be caught up in God's shaking, but instead, we will be miraculously spared.

Even the Greatest Men Need To Repent

The 51st Psalm where David prayed for God's mercy according to His love, was written during David's darkest hour. He had fallen into sin with Bathsheba and murdered her husband indirectly by putting him into the front lines. Uriah was one of David's most loyal generals, yet he had his life taken. I am not talking about some little-known person in the Bible, I am talking about one of the most commanding figures in the Old Testament, one of the greatest kings of Israel.

It does not matter how great you are — when you mess up, you have to repent. When David wrote this psalm, he was overwhelmed with remorse and shame. He was broken by guilt, and in the first line, he calls out for the mercy of God.

The word *blot* in Psalm 51:1 means "to cover up" or "to wash away." *Transgression* means "rebellion." And the Bible says **rebellion is like the sin of divination** (1 Sam. 15:23).

There is a rebelliousness going on. We have been warned — now God is shaking us. But many still are rebellious. They do not want to change. Perhaps a person will go through counseling, or psychiatry, or a drug rehabilitation center. Then pretty soon, he gets that same thing back, because he has not learned to be consistent in the walk of deliverance.

In Psalm 51:2, David said:

> **Wash away all my iniquity** and cleanse me from my sin.

For *iniquity* in that verse, think of the word *perversion*. There is a perverseness in the Body of Christ, a perverted way of thinking about God, about ministry, and about ourselves. I have seen ministers drugged and intoxicated with their own ego and pride, their own selfishness and self-centeredness. They are insensitive to their families and staffs, and they are insensitive to their ministries and to God. They are headstrong and perverted in their thinking.

David got into trouble in the first place because he stayed home at the time of year when kings went off to war. (2 Sam. 11:1.) He was idle, not having enough to do. He was resting on past laurels and successes. That is always dangerous. This is the most idle generation since the days when Rome fell. We do not have enough time for all the time we have! People are restless, hunting for something to do, so they go get a video, go to the movies, watch television, eat, and perhaps end up falling into temptation.

This generation cannot stand silence or the sound of their own thoughts. They have to have the radio or television on — loud! They have to have noise. We have so many available leisure activities in this country, it is like a smorgasbord. There are too many things to choose from and not enough self-discipline. There are Christians whose ministries, marriages, and even lives are out of control. They do not know what to give attention to first, there are so many things wrong. We must have a visitation from God or we will self-destruct.

Stress Is Everywhere

Recently, I found that I had been grinding my teeth at night. I woke up one morning with the right side of my jaw very sore. When I went to the dentist, there was no abscess. The pain was entirely the result of my grinding my teeth in my sleep. I asked him what causes people to grind their teeth at night, and he said, "Stress!"

I thought I was pretty cool about things! Yet here I was grinding my teeth.

The Spirit of God said, "Stress is everywhere. Men under stress. Marriages under stress. Children under stress."

The dentist confirmed this. He told me that his own child grinds his teeth at night, as he also does himself.

"I have to give my child something for his mouth, because there is nothing you can do about it," he said.

What is inside of us that is so pent up? Is it anger? Is it frustration? Is it ambition?

What boils out of people sometimes and causes them to strike someone they love? I have been in churches across the country and seen some of the sweetest-looking couples sitting out there in the congregations. I did not know that perhaps one of those men was beating his wife, destroying her inwardly by bruising her body, and robbing her of dignity, her love for him, and her faith. I did not know that she was scared. And the perpetrator, her husband, was a deacon, an elder, or a pastor.

What are we hiding from? How has the Church gotten so low that we have degraded ourselves and are even lying to ourselves? We do not want to confess the truth, because it is a negative confession.

The Holy Spirit says, "Confess your faults. Confess your sins. Don't say they do not exist. You are grinding your life away."

I began to pray, when I lay my head on the pillow at night: "Jesus, You give Your beloved sleep. (Ps. 127:2) I see myself headed in the direction that too many others have gone. Jesus, I will not do that. Let me rest in peace. Lord, let me have the peace of God in my heart."

What is worrying you is not always something you are doing. It may be something you have done for which you have never repented. That thing is still on your conscience, and the devil is using it against you. You are worried. You are intimidated by that thing, and you are suppressing it. A drug will not cover that. It may be old wounds and hurts, or it may be unforgiveness.

Something happened to me once, and the hurt opened the door for the devil to test me. My heart was really hurting, and I had no one with whom to share it. I am pretty strong most of the time, but in that situation, I was not thinking about anything but my hurt and how to go on in spite of it. I was hurting, but I was not going to let that incident distract me from the ministry.

However, as I drove into my garage and closed the electric door behind me one night, I did something I do not usually do. I sat there in the car with the engine running for a few minutes dealing with the hurt. Usually, I get right out of the car and go into the house.

As I sat there, the devil said to me, "If you ever get to the place where you cannot take it any longer, just sit here with the engine going."

The first thought that came into my mind was, "How dare you? I am going to tell God on you! The idea of a demon telling a man of God to commit suicide! I'm going to tell the people on you. Devil, if you are saying this to me when I am as strong in the Lord as I am, I know you are saying it to my people. I know you are saying it to others. I'm going to warn the people about you!"

And that is what I have been doing and am doing even now.

Christians Must Not Lose the Ark

What causes *Ichabod* (the glory of the Lord is departed) to be written over the door of a church, a nation, a ministry or a person? (1 Sam. 4:21.) *Ichabod* is written over something when man tries to take the glory to himself and God's precious anointing is mishandled.

The Holy Spirit is portrayed in the Gospels as a dove (Matt. 3:16, Mark 1:10, Luke 3:22, and John 1:32), and a dove is a very sensitive bird. If you have ever tried to slip up on one, you will have some idea of what I am talking about. You have to move very carefully, gently, and almost with reverence when you are around a dove. Every move must be deliberate and calculated. One misstep or mistake, and he will be gone.

That is why it is so important that once the presence of God comes into a service, we do not mess things up with our flesh. We must not get flesh mixed in with the anointing, because as quickly as the Holy Spirit comes, He will leave. Not only the ministers in a service, but the musicians, and even the congregation must be very reverent with the anointing. They must carry it a certain way and cover it a certain way in order to keep it.

I do not believe we have to lose the Ark in battle as did Israel in the days of Eli and his wicked sons. I believe we can fight our battles without losing the anointing and without losing God's holy presence in our lives and ministries. We do not have to — and must not — give in to Satan's sinister schemes to undermine the sanctity of the family and the Church.

> *You* will keep in *perfect peace* him whose mind is steadfast, because he trusts in you.
>
> **Isaiah 26:3**

9

The Anointing:

Cover It, Carry It, Keep It

There is only one right — therefore safe — way to carry God's anointing. That way is recorded in Numbers 4:4-6 where God instructed the Kohathite branch of the Levitical priests how to carry the Ark of the Covenant.

The Ark in the Old Testament represented God's presence, power, and protection among His people. The spiritual equivalent since the death and resurrection of Jesus has been the mighty anointing of the Holy Spirit on and in our lives. The Ark today is God testifying of Himself within our hearts.

First, the Ark must be *covered* with holiness. Secondly, the anointing must be *carried* on the shoulders of responsible "priests," men or women; and thirdly, you *keep* the anointing by "hearing and obeying" all of the Lord's commands.

You cannot come into church on Sunday and enjoy the anointing for an hour and a half, then the rest of the week have nothing. In the Spirit, we can walk in God's anointing, the presence of the Holy Spirit, all the time.

Recovering the Ark

Israel lost the Ark in the final days of Eli's priesthood, and it was more than sixty years later before it was regained. We can learn spiritual lessons for our day from the things Israel learned during the recovery of the Ark.

One of David's first objectives as king was to restore the Ark to Jerusalem. David finally was king of all Israel, which had not yet split into two nations, and he wanted the anointing back where it belonged — at the center of the nation's culture and government. The spiritual life of the nation was the focus of the entire country. The apostasy, secularism, and falling away that resulted in the disappearance of Israel and the later captivity of Judah had not yet begun.

David's intentions were good as he set out to restore the anointing back to Israel. He was right in wanting to bring the Ark to Jerusalem and make that city capital of the entire country. However, the Ark had been absent from the nation so long that neither David nor any of the priests remembered God's prescribed manner for carrying the Ark.

They made a new cart to carry it on.

That cart could be called *a cart of compromise,* or a cart of carnality, or a cart of spiritual lethargy (laziness). God had said the Ark was to be carried with special poles *on the shoulders of priests.*

A "cart of spiritual lethargy" seems to be typical of today's men and women of God. Many in the Church seem to be dealing very carelessly and callously with the anointing of the Holy Spirit. They seem to be flippant, almost cocky, in the way they handle sacred things. They praise and worship God but with no sacred regard for holiness.

In my opinion, there is a conspicuous and diabolical conspiracy of silence on the subject of Biblical holiness and sanctification. When the people of God who are called out from the world refuse to separate themselves, we are in trouble. God is demanding from the Church a new and fresh commitment, an anointing of holiness — not bands and choirs, activities, projects, and programs — but a special relationship of holiness unto God. He is wanting a sacred and reverent regard for His relationship with us.

The most dear and treasured thing in my life is the anointing. I desire nothing more than the presence of the Holy Spirit. There is nothing comparable to the anointing. I know of no life apart from the ministry anointed of God. I have no friends apart from the ministry. I have no thoughts, ambitions, or desires apart from being in that special, sacred place in God.

I am not talking about something external. I am talking about something in the deepest recesses of my soul, in my heart of hearts. May I never lose the testimony of God in my life! If I lose every computer, every mailing list, every staff member, every building, may I never lose the anointing. I know what David meant when he said:

> **Do not cast me from your presence or take your Holy Spirit from me.**
>
> **Psalm 51:11**

He also said:

> **Create in me a pure heart, O God, and renew a steadfast spirit within me.**
>
> **Psalm 51:10**

David was so intent on God that Scripture says he was a man after God's own heart. (Acts 13:22.)

When the Holy Spirit came to the Church at Pentecost almost two thousand years ago, what drew the people's attention and made them marvel? They heard them speak in each hearer's own language **the wonderful works of God** (Acts 2:11 KJV). We are hearing too little of the works of God today and too much of the works of men.

Dealing Irreverently With the Anointing

The strength of a church is not in its computers, its mailing lists, its numerical size, or its finances. None of those necessarily carry God's anointing. The strength of a church, a ministry, or a person is in the manifested power and presence of God through the anointing that breaks the yoke of bondage.

The Church has gotten away from allowing God to testify of Himself in our midst. Our spiritual strength is not determined by our ability to manuever politically or socially or to manipulate diplomatically. There is nothing greater than the testimony of God in a church. The wonderful works of men will not last. They will burn as wood, hay, and stubble (1 Cor. 3:12 KJV), but His Words shall not pass away. (Matt. 24:35.)

The sons of Abinadab, Uzzah, and Ahio were guiding the new cart. *Uzzah* means "strength." He probably was a physically commanding person with large muscles and an impressive physique. *Ahio* means "the brother" or "brotherly."[1] David was well-

---

[1]The Bible Almanac, edited by J. I. Packer, Merrill C. Tenney, and William White, Jr. (Nashville: Thomas Nelson Publishers. Copyright (C) 1980), pp. 676, 607.

intentioned as he set out to restore the Ark. Brotherly love was out in front, and physical strength was by his side. David and his thirty thousand chosen men were celebrating with all their might before the Lord. They were dancing and playing instruments. It was a parade with pageantry and beauty. (Many people today know how to *praise* in His presence, but they have never learned how to *practice* His presence.)

> **David and the whole house of Israel were celebrating with all their might before the Lord, with songs and with harps, lyres, tambourines, sistrums, and cymbals.**
>
> **2 Samuel 6:5**

Many times the Spirit of God is falling upon a place, everyone is praising and worshipping God in holiness, and tears are flowing, someone jumps up and says, "Praise Me, praise Me, saith the Lord. Yea, yea, praise Me. I am in your presence."

Sometimes, when the presence of God is on a place, the most immature, unspiritual person in the house wants to give a word, or maybe it is someone with a false spirit who wants to take the attention away from the purity, virtue, and integrity of the Holy Spirit and put it on their flesh. We do not have a lot of false prophets in the Church — just a lot of false prophecies.

Crossing the Threshing Floor

> **When they came to the threshing floor of Nacon, Uzzah reached out and took hold of the Ark of God, because the oxen stumbled.**
>
> **2 Samuel 6:6**

The threshing floor represents a rocky, rough, or unstable ground. When you go through those rocky, rough, and unstable times in life, you will stumble if you are not carrying the anointing properly. When the oxen stumbled, the cart was upset, and the Ark began to slip off. There are men today whose cart is being shaken, and it is causing the anointing to slip and slide. They do not know what to do. In panic, they impulsively *reach out in the flesh* trying to steady the Ark of God's presence in their lives or ministries. Then suddenly they find themselves struck down by God Himself.

You cannot steady the Ark with the arm of flesh, whether it is your marriage, your business, or your church. You must do whatever you do by the Spirit of God. You have to do it the way God wants it done.

The Lord was angry with Uzzah because he dealt irreverently with the Ark. Today, the Lord is angry with His Church because so many have dealt irreverently with the anointing, with His presence.

> The Lord's anger burned against Uzzah because of his irreverent act; therefore God struck him down and he died there beside the ark of God.
>
> 2 Samuel 6:7

God struck Uzzah because he touched sacred things with the flesh, although what he did was "natural." He probably was walking near the cart for the very purpose of steadying it or buttressing it in case it did slip. I am sure he was well-intentioned and basically pure in his motives. However, when it comes to the sacred things of God, there is no excuse for irreverence or human interruptions. He died beside the Ark of God.

You can be walking both in or near the anointing, and because of some inadvertent but irreverent act, be instantly struck down by God. The Ark was not affected, but the one who touched it died instantly. We do not see much of that kind of thing today, but I have a feeling we may see it during the next visitation.

David and the people became afraid of the Lord that day, and three months went by before they dared to try to move the Ark again. They only made another effort after David went back to Jerusalem and looked up the procedures laid down by God to carry the Ark.

> After Aaron and his sons have finished covering the holy furnishings and all the holy articles, and when the camp is ready to move, the Kohathites are to come and do the carrying. *But they must not touch the holy things or they will die.* The Kohathites are to carry those (holy) things that are in the Tent of Meeting.
>
> Numbers 4:15

The "Kohathites" today are the men and women who are called to the ministry to work under the anointing of the Spirit of God. We (the Church in general and ministers in particular) have become that priestly generation. Our responsibility is to take care of *the most holy things.* (Num. 4:5-20.)

The Camp Is Moving

We are moving from one camp to another. The leadership of the last encampment is running its last mile. A few of them may live another ten or twenty years, but most of them will go home to be with the Lord within the next three to five years or their ministries will decline. The Body of Christ is moving into another realm both historically and spiritually.

When the camp was to move, Aaron and his sons would go in and take down the shielding curtain. (Num. 4:5.) Then the priests covered the Ark with the hides of sea cows, spread a cloth of solid blue over that, and put the carrying poles in place. (Num. 4:9-11.)

The Ark was made with gold rings on each corner, and the carrying poles were to be slid through those rings, in order for the Ark to be hoisted up onto the *shoulders* of the priests. That was the way the Ark was to be carried — not on some new cart, not with some new gimmick, and not by some new technology. There is only one way to carry the anointing, and that is on the shoulders of responsible priesthood and responsible holiness.

Carrying the anointing and never touching it with the flesh *is possible.* Those who carry the gifts of the Spirit in their lives, or who carry special talents from God, are not supposed to take hold of those gifts and talents with their flesh and use them for selfish purposes. As a Church, we have to carry the anointing without touching it and without taking any of the glory associated with the Holy Spirit. We have to be able to flow in the Spirit, perform miracles and wonders, cast out devils, and heal the sick — yet never touch the glory or use the anointing to manipulate.

William Seymour, who was greatly used in the Azusa Street outpouring of 1906 and 1907, was a black preacher blind in one eye. He would never come into a service until time to preach. Before he preached, to keep his flesh in check and prevent it from touching God's glory, he would go into a back room, put his head under a box, close his eyes, and pray until time to minister. Also, he often preached with a paper bag over his head because he was so careful about touching the glory or obstructing the anointing with his flesh.

Sometimes at the close of a service when there has been a powerful manifestation of God, I want to stay, shake hands, and hug the people, but the Holy Spirit will say, "Get out of here."

Once I said, "Why? I just want to touch them and enjoy the fellowship for a while."

But God said, "Get out of here, and leave them focusing on Me. If they rush up here and thank you, you are guilty of stealing my glory."

He said, "I will not share the glory."

He will share His love, His gifts, and His grace, but He will not share the glory.

When the Ark was lost in battle during the time of the prophet Eli, seventy men opened up the Ark of the Covenant and looked into it. All of them were struck down immediately and died. (1 Sam. 6:19.) You cannot look at the anointing with the natural eye, touch it with the natural hand, or acquire it through natural means.

The entire Church is pleading, praying, and crying for revival. We are crying out for the harvest, but harvest cannot come until we get to the place where we carry God's anointing properly. God wants to send the rain of His blessings, and that day is soon to come, but if we, in our efforts to "bring back the glory" do not learn how to do so properly, we will be judged by that same glory — and who shall be able to stand?

After three months of studying the scrolls in the temple, David learned how the Ark was to be carried, so he called out the priests. They put the Ark on their shoulders and carried it into Jerusalem, dancing all the way.

A Revival of Holiness

Some of our predecessors may have erred in some way in carrying the Ark, but this generation — 21st century Christianity — *must* go back to the Word of God and find out how to carry the Ark God's way. We must forget the new cart, if we are going to carry the presence of God back to Jerusalem and dance all the way.

The coming move of God is not just going to be miracles, signs, and wonders. This move involves a revival of holiness. People are sick and tired of seeing the loss of integrity, the loss of the anointing, and the yokes not being broken. We may get our cups a quarter filled or sometimes half filled in our churches, but we never seem to get them full to overflowing. The rain is not falling. There is a real, definite drought.

Also, the Baby Boom Generation is not supporting the Church. We are adults with families and businesses, but we will not respond to computer letters. We built those computers! Our parents' generation is moving off the scene after supporting the Church for forty years. My generation needs to respond — yet we are not.

My generation is ready to come back to God, but the Church is not communicating with this age group. This is a generation that wants transparency, realness, humility, integrity, and accountability. However, the Church is caught up in materialism and "gimcrackery." We use gimmicks to raise funds, instead of truth or faith.

My generation backslid, went out, and did its own thing. Now it wants to raise its children in church, but the churches are spiritually bankrupt. The average attendance in churches in America is between fifty and eighty people on a Sunday morning, except in a few very large churches.

Revival is not another Christian television station or program. *Revival* is not another Christian school or building. The revival to come is a holiness that is going to come on us in order to turn our attention toward God and to cause us to re-center on Jesus Christ. We are going to enter into an intimacy and a romance in the Holy Spirit, which is something most Christians have never experienced in their lives.

> Your plunder, O nations, is harvested as by young locusts; like a swarm of locusts men pounce on it.
>
> The Lord is exalted, for he dwells on high; he will fill Zion with justice and righteousness.
>
> He will be the sure foundation for your times, a rich store of salvation and wisdom and knowledge; the fear of the Lord is the key to this treasure.
>
> Isaiah 33:4-6

Right in the midst of the attack of the enemy, right in the midst of famine and drought, the Lord dwells on high. He is the only sure foundation, because everything else is unstable. The only sure foundation for our times is the Lord. Our foundation is not a denomination or credentials. It is not an institution or an affiliation with an organization.

Jesus said:

> ... **On this rock I will build my church, and the gates of Hades** (Hell) **will not overcome it.**
> **Matthew 16:18**

He did not say the "gates of hell" would not be there, nor did He say that we would not have to come against them. But He *did* say they would not be able to stand against us.

The flesh has to die, so the Spirit of God can raise up a vessel that is clean, yielded, and full of the Holy Spirit.

> **Now to him who is able to do immeasurably more than all we ask or imagine, according to his power that is at work within us, to him be glory in the church and in Christ Jesus throughout all generations, for ever and ever! Amen.**
> **Ephesians 3:20,21**

This shaking and purging by fire is preceding the greatest outpouring of the Spirit and power of God that the world has ever known. My generation is not going to be a weak generation. We are going to be a resolute generation in the Church. The Lord is raising up a new breed of Christian, a generation filled with the Holy Spirit and full of discernment, a generation to do exploits for their God.

> The sinners in Zion are terrified; trembling grips the godless; "Who of us can dwell with the consuming fire? Who of us can dwell with everlasting burning?" He who walks righteously and speaks what is right, who rejects gain from extortion and keeps his hand from accepting bribes, who stops his ears against plots of murder and shuts his eyes against contemplating evil — this is the man who will dwell on the heights, whose refuge will be the mountain fortress. His bread will be supplied, and water will not fail him.
>
> Isaiah 33:14-16

He who speaks what is right and rejects gain from the lying manipulations that oppress the people will live on the high places. God is going to take care of our hunger and our needs with the Word. He is going to let the rain fall on us. We are going to have spiritual revival in the midst of all the trouble.

David's wife, Michal, judged and criticized him for the way he danced and worshipped God as the Ark was being brought into the city. *And the judgment that came on her was to have no children.* (2 Sam. 6:23.) Those who judge and criticize the carrying of the anointing back into the Church according to God's way and His direction *will have no spiritual children*. They will be cursed with spiritual barrenness.

The Ark must be carried on the shoulders of responsible priesthood and reverential holiness before the Lord of Hosts. Let us bring it back together worshipping Jehovah God in the beauty of holiness!

10

Separating the Tares From the Wheat

Jesus told them another parable: "The kingdom of heaven is like a man who sowed good seed in his field. But while everyone was sleeping, his enemy came and sowed weeds among the wheat, and went away. When the wheat sprouted and formed heads, then the weeds also appeared.

"The owner's servants came to him and said, 'Sir, didn't you sow good seed in your field? Where then did the weeds come from?'

"'An enemy did this,' he replied.

"The servants asked him, 'Do you want us to go and pull them up?'

"'No,' he answered, 'because while you are pulling the weeds, you may root up the wheat with them. Let both grow until the harvest. At that time I will tell the harvesters: First collect the weeds and tie them in bundles to be burned, then gather the wheat and bring it into my barn.'"

Matthew 13:24-30

A lot of Christians are disillusioned, frustrated, discouraged, and even frightened because they do not understand that separating the wheat from the tares is not just something to occur at the final judgment. On a smaller scale, God is making a separation even today.

Tares are weeds that look like wheat but have poisonous seeds. They look like good grain until the wheat sprouts. Tares and wheat are separated at the harvest. The grain of the tares is smaller and lighter, and most of it will blow away with the chaff of the wheat. But during the growing season, the wheat is hard to distinguish from the tares. Separation before harvest would mean losing some wheat. After the winnowing process, if any tares remain, they are separated from the wheat by being passed through a sieve.

God is in the process of winnowing, and at the same time, passing Christians through a sieve of His holiness and His righteousness. Tares are a symbol of people in churches but also are symbols of things in our lives. Tares are poisonous seeds that affect our fruit.

Passionately Desire To Bear Good Fruit

We not only do not want to lose eternal life, but we should want passionately to bear good fruit in this life. No matter how spiritual you are, there are times when you get sleepy or sluggish (v. 25), then the enemy can slip in and plant tares in your wheat crop.

There are times when my spirit does not want to fight. I do not want to war or to be sober and vigilant. When I preach, pray, work hard at the altar, and minister to the needs of people in a service, then go home to an empty house or hotel room, I am not ready to do spiritual warfare.

Sometimes by the time I leave a service, I am a little "bloody" myself. By the time any minister gets through really preaching and ministering deliverance, he is battle scarred. You are tired, and sometimes your spiritman wants to go to sleep or at least rest. At those times the enemy likes to plant his seed.

A Christian should be good soil, but that means good soil for even the enemy's seeds. *Good soil is good soil.* Tares will not grow among thorns or on rocky ground any more than wheat will. Tares only grow in good soil. If God plants a seed in us, that means we are fertile soil. That seed will take root, germinate, and begin to grow. The same good soil can give growth to bad seeds.

People are confused in the Body today, because they cannot believe bad seeds are growing in Christians right next to good seeds. In this shaking, there are some people who are weeds to be winnowed out, but mostly it is the weeds that will be identified in the good soil of each of us as God puts us through a sieve. God will eliminate those weeds if we allow it, or at least equip us with the wherewithal to conquer them rather than be overcome by them.

Jesus Had No Illusions

Jesus had no illusions about this world or about His Church in it. He did not think the world was going to become a Utopia. He told the disciples before there was a Church that there would be various stages of growth and development and various degrees of receptivity. Some people are not going to grow. Some are not going to mature. Some are not even going to receive the Word.

He explained in parables — examples in story form — that His message was not going to be perfectly received. Sometimes, He explained, the message was not going to be received at all. At other times, the enemy would counterfeit the wheat that was planted. The enemy always has planted tares among the wheat.

The enemy is *the devil*, not your family, your friends, your in-laws, the national government, the IRS, or anybody else. We are fighting each other when we ought to be fighting the sower of bad seeds.

Look at Matthew 13:31-35 where Jesus talked about mustard seed faith and about yeast. "The Kingdom may have small beginnings," is what He was saying. Sometimes the Kingdom may seem weak and small, but like faith, His Kingdom acts as a grain of mustard seed and will increase to a major tree. If we exercise our measure of faith, the Kingdom can increase to a tree in each of our lives. If enough Christians show forth the fruits of the Kingdom, the entire Church could become not only a major tree in the world but a great holy forest of faith.

In most other references, when Jesus talked about *leaven* (yeast), He was using an example of how a little sin can spoil the whole thing. But in this case, He was using *leaven* to point out that the opposite example also is true: a small measure of faith can *leaven* the world. Our mustard seed faith, like a little leaven, can slowly work its way through the whole batch of human society and the world.

I have seen mustard seeds, and they are tiny. But in the Middle East, they can grow into tall, commanding trees with branches birds can land on and take lodging in. He was saying that small drippings of the Kingdom could eventually work themselves through the entire society and eventually reach the whole world.

At that time, the Kingdom for which Israel had looked so long had come in the person of Jesus (Matt. 12:28), but few people really understood Who He was or what He was saying. Even the disciples were getting discouraged. Jesus was warning them that not everyone was going to receive His message in the same way.

Our Tents Are Pitched in Enemy Territory

He said wheat and tares must *grow together* until the harvest. That is the part we do not like. I do not want tares growing *with* me, and I do not want tares growing *within* me — yet they are here. Our tents are pitched in enemy territory. There is a real war going on, both without and within.

I have always said, "Look, people, I am not an angel. We are all in this thing fighting together and trying to make it. Some of us have more success and victory in our lives than others, but ministers are not better than anyone else."

Some people believe that if Jimmy Swaggart could not be perfect and make it, then neither can they. They thought he was the strongest Christian who ever lived. (I am only referring to him by name because his situation has become public knowledge.) But Brother Swaggart is not Jesus, nor is he the Holy Ghost. And *the Holy Spirit and Jesus* did not fail. They did not fall. Our trust must be in Jesus, not in man's example.

Brother Swaggart had tares in his life, more severe than some. Unfortunately, however, his tares are not more severe than those of some others whose tares have *not* been publicly exposed. Jimmy Swaggart had not learned how to deal with his tares, but public exposure forced him to deal with them.

You may wonder, "How can a man so anointed, so powerful in preaching, and so successful in ministry have weeds growing in his life?"

The weeds were there because the harvest had not yet taken place. Now the harvest has begun in him. But many people have taken his situation as reason to give up. They had better wait for the harvest. They need to work out their salvation with fear and trembling and allow the Lord to pull out the weeds.

Some people are married to tares. Others have birthed tares (or terrors) into the world! Some work beside tares in the world and in the ministry. Some people are dealing with tares in their lives that are aggravating and confusing. They may begin to wonder if they really are saved or if they have the Holy Spirit.

"Is the Bible right, or is this all a bunch of fairy tales? How can we live right next to tares, or how can these weeds be growing in us if we are really saved?"

Most of us may not know tares are there until something causes them to surface. I remember the first time I found out I had a temper. I was only seven or eight years of age when temper rose up in me. I overheard a conversation between a girl and her brother on the school bus. I thought they were talking about my sister, but they were not. I was raised with the attitude that you can talk about me but not about my family! I tried to kill that girl! I broke out in a cold sweat and was shaking. My reaction was nothing but the devil, but I did not know tares had been planted in me. I did not know temper was there.

Later, a guy came into our house and began to fight my brother, who could have taken care of himself. But I got a heavy skillet and attacked that guy. So I know what it is like to find a tare in yourself and hate it. I do not know what I would be if I was not full of the Holy Spirit, Who keeps all that stuff at bay.

Don't Judge the End by the Beginning

Jesus talked about the mustard seed and explained how small beginnings can grow up to be something strong and wonderful. In Matthew 13:36-43, He explained in plainer words the parable of the tares to His disciples. Then in verse 44, He approached the explanation of the Kingdom in a different parable.

"The kingdom of heaven is like treasure hidden in a field. When a man found it, he hid it again, and then in his joy went and sold all he had and bought that field.

"Again, the kingdom of heaven is like a merchant looking for fine pearls. When he found one of great value, he went away and sold everything he had and bought it.

Matthew 13:44-46

Responsibility is the other side of privilege. The man did not want the field. He wanted the treasure in the field, but in order to get it, he had to buy the field. He had to buy the rocks, weeds, and everything in the field in order to get the treasure. There is a treasure in the Body of Christ, but you have to buy the field in which it is planted. There are rocks, weeds, tares, gullies, hills, and ravines in the Body which are not pleasant. The higher you go in God, the more pronounced the temptation is, but the more pronounced the resilience can be in you. Rejecting temptation can become easier. Your spirit can rise up against this thing coming at you. We are the *instruments* of righteousness, but the *victims* of decay.

If you hate sin, you have to deal with the tares in your life and not hang on to the idealistic and unrealistic thought that you will never be tempted. You have to learn to live in a world full of beautiful people and not lust after them. You have to learn to live in a world with money and not covet it. You have to live in a world that offers everything imaginable and be able to say no because of the discipline of God. There are temptations, passions, and drives of the flesh, but you have power in the name of Jesus to overcome them.

We need to "sell" everything we have and buy the Kingdom.

The Kingdom Is Like a Net

"Once again, the kingdom of heaven is like a net that was let down into the lake and caught all kinds of fish. When it was full, the fishermen pulled it up on the shore. Then they sat down and collected the good fish in baskets, but threw the bad away. This is how it will be at the end of the age. The angels will come and separate the wicked from the righteous and throw them into the fiery furnace, where there will be weeping and gnashing of teeth."

Matthew 13:47-52

In the verses quoted above, Jesus gave still another analogy of the Kingdom of God. He said the Kingdom is like a net that gathers in all kinds of people. There are different qualities, different styles, different ministries, and so forth in the Kingdom. Jesus — not us — is to distinguish between the good and bad. He does not throw the whole catch out because of a few bad ones. He does not throw the net away or stop fishing. He picks out the bad fish and throws them back.

I remember the first time I ever went deep sea fishing. I kept bringing up eels. Also, I have gone fishing with friends of mine in the crabbing business in the Chesapeake Bay. They would pull up those big nets and there would be twelve to fifteen slithering, slimy eels. But in the middle of all those eels would be several thousand dollars worth of crabs.

My associate pastor, Gary McIntosh, had an interesting experience at his home one day. He went out into his yard to turn on the sprinkler system. As he reached out to turn it on, his hand lit right on top of a large object. When he looked down, he screamed and jumped so high a man a block away began to run toward him.

He had put his hand down on a snake an inch and a half thick. The next thing he knew, he was in the house and still shaking! But he went back outside and to the garage for a long shovel, because every time he turned on the sprinkler system he would be expecting to touch that snake again. So he had to get rid of it. He reached in, pulled it out, and dispatched it.

As he was walking back into the house, the Spirit of God said to him: "The enemy is strategically placing vipers to attack My people."

Satan knows your areas of weakness, and he knows your attitudes and habits. If you are not observant, you will find yourself reaching for a sprinkler system and grabbing a snake.

The Other Side of Privilege Is Responsibility

The children of Israel loved the milk and honey but hated the law and broke it constantly. They loved the miracles, the flow of the anointing, the manifestation, but when it came to the responsibilities, they rejected them repeatedly throughout their history.

The same thing is true today in the Church. We need to begin to walk in the discipline of allowing the tares to be removed from our lives and to face the fact of their removal from our churches. But we also need not throw out the whole net with the bad fish.

If I learn of some blatant, deliberate, open sin in a member of my congregation, I deal with the person involved. I do not *judge* them. I preach judgment, but I do not pass judgment. However, in yourself, you have to judge and deal with sin in any stage.

I have to watch my weight, and I love to eat. I am not a sinner because I have an appetite. But I wrestle or exercise the responsibility of discipline to keep my body under subjection. I wrestle to keep my temper under subjection. I wrestle to keep every desire, every appetite, every hunger under subjection to the Holy Spirit. God has rescued me from, or preserved me through, every test and every trial. The tares are there, but so is Jesus. I am not intimidated by the weeds. I know in whom I have believed.

Don't Neglect the Good Wheat

The enemy will come and plant a seed, and you say, "Where's the culprit?"

He is gone, but the weed is still there. (v. 13.) The seed has been sown and is growing. You are busy looking for the evil sower, but the tares are just growing and growing. While you are chasing the devil, you neglect the good wheat. So you have to learn how to guard the good wheat and not let the tares completely wrap themselves around you and choke out your life.

If I could eradicate all the sinners and all the sin out of the world, out of my church, out of my life, I would do it. If I could make this a Utopia, I would do it, but I cannot. Even God has not done that. But He has given us the ability to deal with sin.

Remember that sin is at first pleasing. The second time, it is easier to commit that same sin. Then committing that sin actually becomes a delight. You begin to look forward to sinning. There is something mysterious and fascinating about sin. Most preachers will not say this. They make sin seem so terrible and so awful — and its consequences are. But in itself, sin usually is very appealing, or we would not be tempted to do it.

The tares I am talking about are not carnal outward sins, but the sins within: pride, ego, backbiting, lust, covetousness, greed, competition, faithlessness, and so forth. First that thing is pleasing, then it is easy, then delightful, and finally frequent. You develop a habit of committing the same sin. Ultimately you become a confirmed sinner, and your attitude changes from one of guilt or conviction to one of defense.

You begin to say, "There is nothing wrong with that. I do not want anybody judging me. Everybody sins. No one is perfect."

Then you get impenitent, which means you have no sense of repentance, and you resolve never to repent. Then you are ruined.

The Apostle John wrote:

> No one who is born of God will continue to sin, because God's seed remains in him; he cannot go on sinning, because he has been born of God. This is how we know who the children of God are and who the children of the devil are: Anyone who does not do what is right is not a child of God; nor is anyone who does not love his brother.
>
> **1 John 3:9,10**

He did not mean we would not commit sin. He meant we could not practice sin.

The Wisdom of the World

Some Christians think they have a corner on the market of God. They know what to do. They know how to do things just right. They are going to manipulate God. About five or six years ago, I sat with a great man of God (and I am *not* talking about

Oral Roberts). This was a great evangelist whom I loved and respected very much.

I said, "Sir, I would like you to share your wisdom with me. I am a young man just getting started. You have a great ministry. Your name is known all over the world. God has used you, and I appreciate you so much. Would you share with me? What should I do?"

The first thing he told me to do was "milk" my mailing list. Buy new lists. Swap the names around. Study "Rev. Ike" a little more and see if I could learn his technique of mottos and little slogans.

He said, "You have a lot of talents and a lot of gifts. We just love you, Carlton. You are just wonderful. You can do this and do that, and you can take the nation by storm. Here is the way you do it."

My heart sank lower and lower. Not once did he mention prayer. Not once did he mention consecration. Not once did he mention godliness. Not once did he mention fasting. Not once did he mention the anointing. He only told me how I could raise money by using the same tactics that the world uses — "the wisdom of the world."

The "wisdom of the world" is chaff.

What Happens to the Chaff?

The chaff that was left after threshing and winnowing was partly dirt, partly the hard, inedible coat of the outer shell of the grain, and partly any tares that had been mixed in with the harvest. The wind is going to drive away the chaff from our lives. Most of the people who run around talking about the baptism of the Holy Spirit concentrate on speaking in tongues. They do not know the baptism also is to sanctify you, separate you, blow all the chaff out of your life. I am tired of people speaking in tongues while living ungodly lives.

God's winnowing fork is in His hand, and He is going to toss the saints up in the air in the wind of the Spirit. Get ready, because if you take it, it will blow the chaff out of your life. The dust and dirt will be blown away. If you are tired of wrestling with these same old stupid, carnal sins, let God toss you into the wind.

Barley and wheat were the two largest, most important grain crops in the Middle East, and grain was the last of the harvest. The harvest lasted for seven weeks, from Passover to Pentecost — fifty days. Entire families moved out of their homes to live in the fields until the harvest was over.

Today, entire church families are going to have to move out of their settled "homes," out of the little, quaint church structures and get into the field to stay there until harvest is over. Instead of sending checks to the fields, we are going to have to go ourselves. We need to leave the comfort zone for the fields.

In the past great revivals, it has been impossible to prevent "wildfire" (false manifestations of the supernatural, or manifestations from familiar spirits) from getting mixed in with the true fire of the Holy Spirit. The tares were being sown in the field of the Church along with the wheat, but praise God, the wheat remained.

Now is *not* the time to give up on the Body of Christ, the Church. The problem is that we want instant results and instant answers. But it takes time to be holy. It takes time to be consistent. The tares are there, but *let God be God*. I am not going to let the devil choke out the Kingdom in me. I am not going to let the deceitfulness of riches choke out the message in me. I am not going to be stony or shallow ground. I am going to be good soil. How about you?

11
Carriers of the Ark

But you are a chosen people, a royal priesthood, a holy nation, a people belonging to God, that you may declare the praises of him who called you out of darkness into his wonderful light. Once you were not a people, but now you are the people of God; once you had not received mercy, but now you have received mercy.

Dear friends, I urge you, as aliens and strangers in the world, to abstain from sinful desires, which war against your soul. Live such good lives among the pagans that, though they accuse you of doing wrong, they may see your good deeds and glorify God on the day he visits us.

1 Peter 2:9-12

We are now the carriers of the Ark, the responsible priesthood, God's treasured possession, a peculiar people, and a chosen generation. We have the sacred responsibility and trust of carrying the Ark in the form of a spiritual anointing. The Church now has an anointing but not anything like it will be in the next few years.

There will be more of the external miracles of God, but we need God to do something inside us first. God must do spiritual work in our lives to prepare us as His vessels to carry the anointing. We need to be holy, pure, sanctified, and separated unto God.

There is a lot of junk in the Church, but there are many people who are desperately hungry for holiness. There are a lot of sinners, half-steppers, and hypocrites, but the majority of people in the churches really want holiness. However, holiness is not being preached from many pulpits. Ministers are afraid of losing their crowds. They are afraid of offending someone. When you preach holiness, however, you really do not offend anyone but the devil.

People want godliness, they want direction, they want leadership. God is looking for men and women who will get down to business, stand their ground, and say, "We are going to carry this anointing, and we are going to do it right. It can be done in holiness, and we are going to do it in holiness."

When the Israelites began to bring up the Ark, as we saw in a previous chapter, they trusted physical strength to guide it. During the past several years, we have seen too much physical, political, financial, manipulative, human strength carrying the anointing.

There is only one way to carry the anointing, and that is on the shoulders of responsible, consecrated priests. That is us, as I have said. We are that Kohathite nation now. We have become the "sons of Aaron." The first responsibility of a priest is to minister to God, and secondly, to his neighbor.

The Beginning Seeds of Revival

Beginning in 1987, I believe, there was planted by God the seeds of a revival, the seeds of a harvest of souls. But as we have seen, before every great move of God, there is a great humiliation. There is a time of earthquakes, wars, or famine that brings people to their knees. People become desperate for help from God, and they pray.

With all of our teaching about the authority of the believer and the prosperity of the saints, I believe somehow the devil mixed into that a spirit of arrogance and pride which has weakened the thrust of the message. Because we did not receive it humbly, we now have to be called back into humility across the threshing floor.

The Place of Jezreel

One day, as I was thinking about the problems of the Church, the Holy Spirit spoke in my heart — "a house of ill repute."

I said, "What are you talking about? Certainly you're not talking about the house of God."

He said, "Yes, My house has become a house of ill repute."

Houses of ill repute are not new. They have been around almost since mankind has been on earth. But I did not like the idea of there being any similarity between houses of prostitution and the Church. However, the Lord showed me that even in Tulsa, where so many ministries are headquartered, God has given us all kinds of indications, all kinds of warnings that the Church has made His Body a house of ill repute. Then the Holy Spirit drew my attention to the book of Hosea where God told a prophet to marry a prostitute!

God raised up a man and put a fiery word in his mouth, and the man's ministry lasted more than forty years. During that time, he had to live with that woman in her condition in order to draw God's people to repentance. All through these books of the prophets, particularly in Isaiah and in some of the minor prophets, God kept pleading for repentance and promising restoration.

I said, "Lord, my audience is so small, just a few hundred or a few thousand. Why don't you give this message to someone else who has a larger audience? What kind of repentance are you asking for?"

He again drew my attention to Hosea:

> So he married Gomer daughter of Diblaim, and she conceived and bore him a son.
>
> Then the Lord said to Hosea, "Call him Jezreel, because I will soon punish the house of Jehu for the massacre at Jezreel, and I will put an end to the kingdom of Israel.
>
> "In that day I will break Israel's bow in the Valley of Jezreel."
>
> **Hosea 1:3-5**

Jezreel is a place of judgment. Jehu's acts of judgment against the house of Ahab and Jezebel took place at Jezreel in a bloody massacre. (2 Kings 9,10.)

What God said to Hosea was, "Name the first child born of your prostitute wife 'Judgment.' I am going to pronounce judgment on my own people. I am going to stop what is happening in My nation."

Today, He is saying, "I am going to stop what is happening in My Church."

The Church has become a house of ill repute, but God is beginning to clean her up. He is sanctifying and separating His people. The Lord showed me last winter how we can last. I have a tree outside my house in Tulsa, and right in the dead of winter, it was green and lush. I looked around, and every other tree was leafless and barren.

I said, "Lord, what is it? What is going on?"

He said, "If you will do what I tell you to do, your 'tree' can last. It can be lush and green right in the time of the famine, in time of winter."

I have a whirlpool out back, and I keep it around 110 degrees. What had happened was that it had warmed the roots of the tree close to it so that the tree never knew it was winter.

God said, "Take care of your roots."

Many of you are covering the top of the tree, but you need to look at the roots. Take care of the roots through prayer. Make sure they are warmed and massaged so that when the ground around them freezes, your roots will be warmed enough for the tree to last right through the dead of winter.

Even though God has blessed us with prosperity, we must remain humble. You know an humble person when you are around him. You can feel the humility that comes forth. God is getting the glory. They are decreasing while He is increasing. I have attended ministers' meetings where only those with more than a thousand members and a nationally recognized ministry were invited. Not from everyone, of course, but from many there was a general spirit of pride and ministerial arrogance.

Men would get up and give glowing reports on the "secret" to having big churches or ministries. They were not speaking of the wonderful works of God as the disciples did on the day of Pentecost. They were speaking of the wonderful works of men. Man was getting the glory. Since then, there has been a conspicuous, though subtle, appearance of the word *Ichabod* over many ministries. The glory of the Lord has departed. Men lost the anointing, lost the Ark, as they crossed the threshing floor.

God's Winnowing Fork Is in His Hand

John the Baptist preached about baptisms, and there is coming a new one today, the baptism with fire.

> "I baptize you with water for repentance. But after me will come one who is more powerful than I, whose sandals I am not fit to carry. He will baptize you with the Holy Spirit, and with fire. His winnowing fork is in his hand, and he will clear his threshing floor, gathering the wheat into his barn and burning up the chaff with unquenchable fire."
>
> **Matthew 3:11,12**

We have heard much teaching on the baptism of the Holy Spirit in the past twenty years, but I have yet to hear a speaker deal with the subject of the winnowing fork. That omission is how the devil has brought deception. In all of the books, clinics, seminars, sessions, and conferences on the Holy Spirit, there has been very little reference to the fire which purifies. They just talk about tongues.

The winnowing fork is in operation any time God clears His threshing floor, gathers His wheat into the barn, and burns up the chaff with unquenchable fire. *That is the reason for the fire: to burn up the chaff.* The baptism of the Holy Spirit comes with fire. Chaff is a mixture of dust, dirt, and the outer shells of the grain. He takes this fork and tosses the grain into the air. The wind (the Holy Spirit), blows the chaff away. Later it is bound and burned.

To get to this coming revival, we are going to have to cross that threshing floor because there can be no harvest without it. That is how the holy are separated from the unholy, the pure from the impure, the light from the darkness. God is purging His Church in a true baptism in fire.

The first thing to happen in the coming revival will be a blanket of God's glorious holiness falling on the church, and through that will come the miracles. We have had "anointings" to build buildings, go on television, build water parks, and build churches, but we have no real anointing for casting out cancers and devils. Pastors are having nervous breakdowns. Their marriages are falling apart. Their kids are going on drugs. There are all types of illicit sex and promiscuity in the Body of Christ. We forgot holiness while we prospered.

To thresh means "to trample out, to tread upon or tread out." When grain was harvested in Bible days, they took rods or flails, a kind of whip, and beat the sheaves to get rid of the tares and the chaff. Or they might have oxen trample them underfoot, then the wind would blow away the chaff.

As you cross the threshing floor, you are going to have to allow the sheaves to be beaten and flailed.

That is why we preach fasting and prayer. I afflict (humble) my soul with fasting. (Ps. 35:13.) In order to humble yourself before God and allow yourself to be molded into God's desire, there will be an afflicting of the soul, humbling both mind and body.

Not many people are preaching this. Instead, it is being preached that God is love; therefore, He will not do anything but bless. He will not flail. Yet the Word says that whom He love; therefore He chastens. (Heb. 12:6 KJV.) That means if God does not chasten you, you are not His child. Children who have been physically abused doubt their parents' love — but so do those who are *never* corrected! One extreme is as bad as the other. God has to deal with us to get us in shape for what is coming.

Thieves Come to the Threshing Floor

Another thing about the threshing floor is that it was hard, usually clay, soil. And since thieves would visit there at harvest time, laborers slept at the threshing place all night to protect the harvest. During this harvest, robbers are going to try to steal from the Body of Christ, especially from those who are not willing to be threshed. There will be soft talkers, sweet talkers, teachers for their itching ears. Those who refuse to submit to the threshing are going to be stolen away. The Bible says there is coming a day when people will not endure sound doctrine.

> For the time will come when men will not put up with sound doctrine. Instead, to suit their own desires, they will gather around them a great number of teachers to say what their itching ears want to hear.
>
> 2 Timothy 4:3

Some people say: "Don't give me the truth. Don't thresh me. Don't whip me. Just tell me how I can get things from God. Tell me how I can be blessed. Tell me how God wants to smile on me, and how wonderful I am, and how precious I am, and how I am supposed to prosper and all the good things. But do not give me truth. Give me milk, porridge, and mush. Don't give me meat, because I do not want to have to chew."

Whole families would leave their homes and spend their time on the threshing floor during the harvest. There is coming a time during this next move of God when His true laborers will have to spend their time doing this threshing. Entire churches and ministries will lay on God's threshing floor of purging.

Threshing floors, if possible, were built high on a hill where the strong winds, the night winds, could more easily blow away the chaff. There is a higher place where this threshing of God takes place. You are going to have to climb up to that higher place where the wind can blow through. The Spirit of God needs to blow again with the sound of a mighty, rushing wind.

Brothers, I could not address you as spiritual, but as worldly — mere infants in Christ. I gave you milk, not solid food, for you were not yet ready for it.

Indeed, you are still not ready. You are still worldly. For since there is jealousy and quarreling among you, are you not worldly? Are you not acting like mere men?

1 Corinthians 3:1-3

Planters and Waterers

We are spending a lot of time today "name dropping." We have to get away from that. Paul said they were still worldly in the Corinthian church because one was saying "I follow Paul," and another, "I follow Cephas." (1 Cor. 1:12.) Today, are we not acting like mere men also?

If you slip around to someone and say, "Brother, they don't let you talk as much, but we really like to hear you," you are stroking that man's ego. You are feeding a part of him that does not need feeding. People said that to me when I was working at the Oral Roberts Evangelistic Association. But I was not worried about whether they let me talk. God was using me where He wanted me. That was the point.

Paul said he planted the seed, Apollos watered it, but God gave the increase. God made it grow. (1 Cor. 3:7b). God gets the glory for the growth of the seed, and the harvest is His. You and I can do nothing more than plant or water. We do not have the power to make anything grow. Then Paul said, *So neither he who plants nor he who waters is anything* (1 Cor. 3:7a).

One of the reasons our church and ministry is growing is because God shows me how to listen. I am making it a little bit at a time just like you. I feel my way along just like the rest of the Church. I simply try to hear God. I strain my ears for Him way in the night when it is real quiet, when the phones have stopped, and everything is silent. Then I am listening.

Actually, I listen to God all the time. When I meet a stranger, I am listening. Someone may make a comment, or I might hear God through reading a book or watching television. I always have my ears atuned and this question in the front of my mind: "Is God saying anything?" Perhaps it is a phone call, overhearing a conversation on an airplane, in a terminal, in a hotel, or through other people's sermons. Perhaps there is a word of encouragement, a revelation, or a word of advice that God will quicken to my spirit through my natural ears. I want to hear from heaven.

The man who plants and the man who waters have one purpose, and each will be rewarded according to his own labor.

> **For we are God's fellow workers; you are God's field, God's building.**
>
> **By the grace God has given me, I laid a foundation as an expert builder ... .**
> **1 Corinthians 3:9,10a**

Paul was not bragging, because the foundation he was talking about laying was Jesus. He simply told everyone he could about Jesus. Then when that person received Jesus, he received a foundation. Paul said:

> **... and someone else is building on it. But each one should be careful how he builds. For no one can lay any foundation other than the one already laid, which is Jesus Christ.**
> **1 Corinthians 3:10**

The one foundation has been laid. Paul said whatever is built on the foundation will be found to be gold, silver, or precious stones, or wood, hay, or straw — *depending on how it comes through the fire.* (1 Cor. 3:13.)

> His work will be shown for what it is,
> because the Day will bring it to light. It will be
> revealed with fire, and the fire will test the quality
> of each man's work.
>
> 1 Corinthians 3:13

When the baptism of the Holy Spirit and fire comes along, with it will come a revelation of what each person is and what he has built. If what he has built survives, he will receive a reward. If what he has built is burned up, he will suffer loss. He himself will be saved, but only as one escaping through the flames. (1 Cor. 3:15.)

Here is a very important point: A lot of ministries are going to be threshed, *but do not judge the leader.*

If the ministry is not built on a solid foundation, if it is built on flesh or manipulation or pride, if it is built on ego, if it is built on competition, if it is built on vindictiveness, it is going to be burned up.

The man who made the error may escape, but it will be like escaping through flames. He will go on to heaven, but there will be no ministry when he is gone. This is going to happen whether we like it or not. The fire is coming.

Wrestling With God

The story of Jacob and Esau is one of the most intriguing of the Old Testament narratives. Not only because it deals with the subject of sibling rivalry with which so many of us are familiar, but more so because of that fascinating wrestling match with God.

The word *wrestled* as used in the passage where Jacob encountered the angel is not the word we understand as wrestling today. (Gen. 32:22-32.) Instead, the real meaning is "to bring to dust or to pulverize" as in grappling or grinding. According to the creation narrative in Genesis, ashes, powder, or dust is the stuff of our fleshly origins and our earthly nature. *Wrestling* in Genesis 32:22 represents a pulverizing or grinding up of the pre-regenerate Adamic nature.

In the coming revival with its mighty outpouring of life-changing and heart-altering power, there will be a rebirthing of, and in, the Church worldwide. The carnal vulnerability of our present condition will be gloriously pulverized even as Jacob's was through his midnight wrestling match with the Angel of the Lord.

The tares *will* be removed by the baptism of fire.

12

The Two Altars of Jacob

Jacob and his twin brother, Esau, were the sons of Isaac and Rebekah and the grandsons of Abraham and Sarah. Rebekah, their mother, like Sarah, their grandmother, had been barren. After years of prayer and petitioning, God granted Rebekah her desire, and she became pregnant.

One day while well along in her pregnancy, she felt a jostling (wrestling) in her stomach. (Gen. 25:22.) The relationship between the brothers that manifested later was established in their mother's womb. Somewhat alarmed by the wrestling within her, Rebekah inquired of the Lord as to what it meant.

His response in Genesis 25:23 was that two *natures* were in her womb and two *purposes* would be separated from within her. One people (Israel) would be stronger than the other (Edomites), and the older (Esau) would serve the younger (Jacob).

When the twins were born, Esau was first.

> **After this, his brother came out, with his hand grasping Esau's heel; so he was named Jacob.**
> **Genesis 25:26**

The literal meaning of *Jacob* is "he grasps the heels," however, the figurative meaning is "he deceives." Other meanings are "supplanter, trickster, liar, manipulator," and so forth.[1] Those names were an indicator of Jacob's nature. The prophecy given to Rebekah was that the older would serve the younger. God had blessed Jacob before he and his mother stole Esau's birthright. Jacob did not need to trick his father. However, Rebekah tried to "help God out," and Jacob's nature was to take advantage of others. Although blessed of God, he had an unregenerate nature.

Despising the Birthright

After the two grew up, Esau was a hunter and Jacob a "home boy." One day, having eaten little or nothing at all before leaving on a hunt probably before daybreak, Esau came back to camp famished. He was desperate for food, which made him more vulnerable to Jacob's manipulation. Jacob did not initiate the selling of the birthright, but he *took advantage* of his brother's needs. (Gen. 25:29-34.) Does that sound like some Christians today?

Esau represents the carnal spirit of ungodly compromise. Because of his lust for food (human appetites), he squandered his very birthright. His sin was identical with Adam and Eve's in the Garden of Eden, though not as devastating. Adam and Eve lost *our* birthright by yielding to Satan.

Apparently, Esau only lived for the moment. He exercised his free will irresponsibly. He apparently was devoid of Godly principles or concern for the importance of his inheritance. In the providence of God, Esau was made subservient to Jacob. In

---

[1]All meanings of names in this chapter are from *The Bible Almanac*, edited by Packer, Tenney, and White.

Hebrews 12:16,17, he is described as a "profane" person. Long after Esau's death, the Lord declared He loved Jacob and hated Esau. (Mal. 1:2,3.) The Apostle Paul used this passage in Malachi to illustrate how God carries out His purposes regardless of the hindrances of man. (Rom. 9:10-13.)

Jacob's nature was hidden behind his handsome and hairless face and his externally mild temperament. Inside, he grabbed, grasped, and grappled with everything and everybody, even God. That same nature manifests in many Christians — pastors and other spiritual leaders included. Outwardly, they appear to be mild-mannered, placid, and tranquil servants of God. Inwardly, they compete, connive, and conspire with the drive and ambition of the most ruthless business tycoon.

My friend James Robison calls these Christians public successes, but private failures. The Church is full of them, and I believe God is about to "wrestle down" that spirit in us, grinding and pulverizing it into dust and powder so the holy wind of His Spirit can blow it away into the abyss where it belongs.

We must not despise our birthright as children of God and trade it for a mess of the world's potage. If we despise our birthright, we will lose the blessings of God as well.

Loss of Blessing Follows Loss of Birthright

After taking advantage of Esau's hunger and weakness to get the birthright, Jacob conspired with his mother some years later to steal his older brother's blessing as well. The consequences were that Jacob had to leave home in a hurry because of fear that his actions would cause Esau to murder him. (Gen. 27.) Up to this point, Jacob apparently felt no remorse or guilt — even when he stopped at Bethel to pray. When I see the extent to which some genuinely God-called people go to fulfill ungodly and selfish ambitions, I am astonished at the conspicuous lack of remorse or godly sorrow.

James wrote about this attitude in the early Church.

> **What causes fights and quarrels among you? Don't they come from your desires that battle within you? You want something but don't get it. You kill and covet, but you cannot have what you want. You quarrel and fight. You do not have, because you do not ask God. When you ask, you do not receive, because you ask with wrong motives, that you may spend what you get on your pleasures.**
>
> **James 4:1-3**

A lot of Christians apparently feel the "end justifies the means." But that is a very dangerous and deceptive attitude. Because of it, many a great man or a great ministry has been destroyed. One day a few years ago, while into one of my periodic times of fasting and prayer, I spent several hours watching a number of television programs on a Christian station.

I still remember the Holy Spirit speaking into my heart this lament, "I am *for* just about every ministry effort you are seeing on your TV set, but unfortunately, I am not *in or with* very much of it. I am for just about every Christian church you see in the world, but again, I'm not *in or with* many of them."

I wept as I asked God why. My spirit heard Him answer, "They will not let Me in their churches or in their plans and programs. Most of them discover what I want and then race ahead to do it without My anointing, or without even seeking My counsel or blessing."

God will not be where He is not wanted nor where He is not welcomed. He does not need our help, *but He desires our cooperation*. The battle really is the Lord's. (2 Chron. 20:15.)

Ambition Can Extinguish the Flame of God

After fleeing from Esau and while enroute to his uncle's house in Haran, Jacob had a divine visitation through a dream. He saw a stairway leading up to heaven, and angels were moving up and down this stairway. Above the stairway stood the Lord. God spoke to Jacob and made him an incredible promise. You would think Jacob would never trust his flesh again. But the story of his life proves differently. Just like Jacob, there are people today with an unmistakable call and anointing of God who allow carnality and fleshly ambition to smother, and sometimes almost extinguish, the flame of God in their lives and ministries.

Two years before Jim and Tammy Bakker fell into disgrace, I appeared on the PTL program when they were hosts. I had made appearances there from 1975 on the program and on the live campmeeting shows. Up until the mid-80s, however, I never spent any personal time alone with either of them. However, on this particular trip, I was awakened at 5:15 a.m. the day I was to be a guest. It did not take me long to discern, even at that early hour, that the Lord wanted to speak to me. I picked up a pen and piece of paper from the nightstand and wrote what God gave me. I did not realize until the next day that the message was for Jim to hear.

After being in the ministry as long as I have, I am well aware of the continuous stream of people who have a "word from the Lord" and try to get close to Christian leaders. I had experienced enough of that myself to avoid being categorized as one of "that kind." However, when the word *really* is from God, there usually is not any trouble delivering it — *if you let Him arrange it.*

At any rate, the Lord opened the door for me to deliver the word from Him. Tammy started a conversation that led right into sharing what the Lord had given me. After hearing it, she asked me to share it with Jim in his private dressing room after that day's program. As best I can recall, this is what the Lord said:

"There are *men of great faith*, and there are *great men of faith*. Men of great faith *do* great things, such as building churches, schools, ministries, and so forth. But great men of faith *become* great things in God, through displaying and exhibiting His character and the nature of His holiness, His humility, and His love."

I went on to say, "Jim, the ministry here has dwarfed the minister, and you're being buried. The ministry is growing, but you're shrinking. You are becoming a midget in your own mansion."

I begged him to let God salvage his life, even if it meant abdicating some of his dreams. Needless to say, he did not listen. In fact, he barely looked at me the entire time I talked, only occasionally glancing up. I had not gone in there with a self-righteous attitude. I loved Jim and Tammy then; I love them now. But I left his dressing room in grief and tears and did not return until a year after he resigned.

The "Jacob" Spirit

We are given an interesting insight into the real nature of Jacob in his response to God after the first visitation at Bethel. This insight can help us understand some of today's leaders in the Church.

The statement **surely the Lord is in this place, and I was not aware of it** (Gen. 28:16) is a basic ingredient of a "Jacob spirit." People with this kind of spirit do not recognize the presence of God. Physically, they are alert, but their spiritual senses are asleep. Their flesh and minds are active — in most cases, too active.

The term *house of God* in verse 17 is another way of saying *will of God*. Through this dream, God was attempting to reveal His will to Jacob, and Jacob recognized God's presence but apparently did not understand the purpose of His presence. The "Jacob spirit" recognizes God's presence but usually misses the purposes of God in his life and calling.

The first part of Genesis 28:17 says that *he was afraid,* and the Hebrew word there could mean either reverence or dread. I believe it was a bit of both. Another basic characteristic of the "Jacob spirit" is that he usually reverences God, but *dreads Him too.*

The "Jacob spirit" does not like to give up control, but grabs and guides and almost never yields or follows. The "Jacob spirit" has an enormous ego.

In Genesis 28:18 and 19, we read how Jacob made the first of two very significant altars in his life. He poured oil on it, and named it *Beth-el* (House of God), indicating his recognition of the "presence of God." He changed the name of the place but did not change his own name. It is obvious that Jacob — and not God — was still in control of his own life.

In the vow he made to God, look how many times the term "me" and "I" appears. Can you believe his prayer? *"Give me, be with me, watch over me," and only after all that would he give God a tenth. Was God his shield and buckler or his shield and butler?* Jacob apparently saw God as a kind of cosmic bellhop or heavenly Santa Claus, to put it in modern terms. Many with "Jacob spirits" feel the same way. If God fulfills their "give me's," then they will "tip" God a tenth of all he gives them!

There was no real reverence, no humility, and no gratitude in Jacob's prayer. That attitude is much too common among God's people today, especially among preachers and spiritual leaders, sad to say. The opposite of *love* is not always *hate*, but "selfishness." A person is not selfish if he pursues his own interests; he is selfish if he neglects everyone else's.

Pay Day Is Coming After a While

The Apostle Paul wrote:

> **Be not deceived; God is not mocked: for whatsoever a man soweth, that shall he also reap.**
> **Galatians 6:7** KJV

Iverna Tompkins, a favorite visiting speaker at my church, says, "If you do not hate the sin in your own life and deal directly with it, God will surround you with people or circumstances that remind you so much of your exact sin that you ultimately grow to hate it and to see it as it is — 'utterly sinful.'" (Rom. 7:13.)

Jacob went to someone who was better at manipulating and conniving than he was. His Uncle Laban got the better of him for a number of years. I think this was another attempt on God's part to cause Jacob to see the error of his ways and to get him to change. Jacob worked for Laban twenty years: fourteen for his wives, Leah and Rachel, and another six for his flocks. (Gen. 31:41.) Then he went back to the land of his father, Isaac.

Jacob now had two wives, eleven sons (the twelfth was born during the journey), some daughters, dozens of servants, large flocks of sheep, goats, cattle, and vast amounts of other accumulated wealth. During the past twenty years, the blessings of his birthright had become exceedingly apparent, and he was a very wealthy man.

He was on his way home to his father Isaac's house, near the place where he had his first visitation with God and where he had built his first altar. He should have been quite happy and full of joy, but he was not. Instead, he was full of fear and distress. He had just received word that Esau was headed toward him with what he thought were four hundred angry menservants. Jacob thought Esau was coming to take revenge on him for his actions twenty years before.

He was miserable and afraid. He wanted to go home, back to where he first recognized the "house" (will) of God for his life. However, he thought his life was in jeopardy because of the wrath of his older brother. In this agonizing moment in his life, Jacob needed some time alone, so he sent his entire family and entourage, probably numbering hundreds of people, on ahead. Verse 24 says Jacob was alone.

> So Jacob was left alone, and a man wrestled with him till daybreak. When the man saw that he could not overpower him, he touched the socket of Jacob's hip so that his hip was wrenched as he wrestled with the man. Then the man said, "Let me go, for it is daybreak."
>
> But Jacob replied, "I will not let you go unless you bless me."
>
> The man asked him, "What is your name?"
>
> "Jacob," he answered.
>
> Then the man said, "Your name will no longer be Jacob, but Israel, because you have struggled with God and with men and have overcome."
>
> Jacob said, "Please tell me your name."
>
> But he replied, "Why do you ask my name?" Then he blessed him there.
>
> So Jacob called the place Peniel, saying, "It is because I saw God face to face, and yet my life was spared."
>
> The sun rose above him as he passed Peniel, and he was limping because of his hip. Therefore to this day the Israelites do not eat the tendon attached to the socket of the hip, because the socket of Jacob's hip was touched near the tendon.
>
> Genesis 32:24-32

A Blessing Beyond the Birthright

As Jacob, all alone now, nervously paced back and forth, to and fro, up and down, his mind probably raced as he prayed. Before he could get his last word out, as I imagine the scenario, someone jumped on him from behind a bush. He was startled and may have thought Esau had taken a short cut and was already upon him. As his character is revealed in the Bible, he probably did not fight fair. He probably screamed, yelled, maybe cursed like a maniac. God was at work making Jacob see himself as he really was, and just as Jacob, in his fright and despair, would have given up, God caused him to know Who he was really resisting and Who he was really up against. Jacob was dusted, powdered, and pulverized into submission. He hung on anyway, wanting more.

He said, "I won't turn you loose unless you bless me."

What? Another blessing? Who does this guy think he is? The nerve of him! He already has the family birthright and blessing. He is rich. What more could he want? *Is there a blessing beyond the birthright?*

To Jacob's request, God asked him a stunning question: "What is your name?" There was a long pause, the kind of silence so loud you can hear it. Why did God ask that? The question goes deeper than it sounds. God was not just asking his name, but, "What is your nature? What is your character? Of what spirit are you?" and finally, "What is the condition of your soul?"

163

Jacob had to confess who he really was. His answer was, "My name is Supplanter, Trickster, Deceiver, Manipulator. My name is Jacob." We all need to look at our own "names" and ask ourselves those questions: What is my name? Has it ever been changed? What is my nature? Have I ever been wrestled into submission?

Before the next great move of God, He is going to change a lot of his people. You will see the dust and ashes flying, you may hear the yells and screams, but let it happen. God is at work in our midst. He loves his people, and our greatest days are still ahead of us. Meanwhile there is a lot to be done in us and on us before those greater things can happen through us.

After Jacob confessed to his nature, the angel who is also referred to as "the Lord," changed his name from Jacob to Israel (v. 28.) The NIV translated the explanation behind this name change this way: **You have struggled with God and with men and have overcome.** In some translations, the term "prince" is substituted for *Israel*, and sometimes the word "priest."

If we assume that the term "priest" also was in God's thinking in naming Jacob *Israel*, it would not be at all unreasonable to tie the "priesthood" into God's call upon Jacob or upon his descendants in general. Old Testament Israel was called a *kingdom of priests* (Ex. 19:6), and New Testament Israel (the Church) is referred to as a *royal priesthood* (1 Pet. 2:9). A king ministers *for* God, whereas a priest ministers *to* God. Kings rule, priests serve.

Jacob appears to have been born with a "kingly anointing," but in order to completely fulfill God's extended purpose in and for his life, he was given a "priestly anointing." The priestly anointing will be the norm within the Body in the coming revival in order for a new generation of men and women to be established who **know their God will firmly resist** (Dan. 11:32) the antichrist spirit of the 21st century.

Peniel: Face of God

Jacob's last altar was named *Peniel*, because, "... **I saw God face to face and still my life was spared**" (Gen. 32:30). At Bethel, he said, "**Surely the Lord is in this place, and I was not aware of it**" (Gen. 28:16). At Peniel, Jacob had a direct and definite encounter with the *person* of God, not just the *presence* of God. That is to say, Jesus wrestled with Jacob, and in so doing, changed his life forever.

He may have been limping that next morning (Gen. 32:25), but he certainly was not the same man. As God begins to change names and natures throughout the Body of Christ, we are going to be seeing quite a few limping preachers and ministries. Some are going to be crippled for longer periods than others, and some will never walk the same way again, nor will they *be* the same. Some will see God face to face and not live. They will be taken home to glory, having lost their usefulness on earth. There *will* be a shake-up before the rain comes, but God will be orchestrating the whole thing.

The only reason the crippling had to take place was that Jacob would not have surrendered before his hip socket was touched. Some people are so unsubmissive and have such stubborn and unyielded wills that even the Lord will not overpower them. But wrestling with Him weakens their mobility and makes them dependent on something or Someone other than themselves.

Such was the case with Jacob, and such will be the case with many modern-day Jacobs scattered throughout the worldwide Body of Christ until we are all walking the same walk and talking the same talk, and **until we all reach unity in the faith and in the knowledge of the Son of God and become mature, attaining to the whole measure of the fullness of Christ** (Eph. 4:13).

At least in one other place in the Old Testament someone claimed to have "seen the Lord" and described the effect the encounter had on him.

> **In the year that King Uzziah died, I saw the Lord seated on a throne, high and exalted, and the train of his robe filled the temple. Above him were seraphs, each with six wings: With two wings they covered their faces, with two they covered their feet, and with two they were flying.**
>
> **Isaiah 6:1,2**

> **"Woe to me!" I cried. "I am ruined! For I am a man of unclean lips, and I live among a people of unclean lips, and my eyes have seen the King, the Lord Almighty."**

> **Then one of the seraphs flew to me with a live coal in his hand, which he had taken with tongs from the altar. With it he touched my mouth and said, "See, this has touched your lips; your guilt is taken away and your sin atoned for."**

> **Then I heard the voice of the Lord saying, "Whom shall I send? And who will go for us?"**

And I said, "Here am I. Send me!"
Isaiah 6:5-8

King Uzziah represented the "old generation" of leadership in Israel, and Isaiah represented the new. According to the first chapter of Isaiah, he had been ministering for several years before Uzziah died, but as the sixth chapter shows, up until the year of the king's death, Isaiah had not really seen the Lord.

There are many people in ministry who have never really seen the Lord, which is to say they do not *know* God. They have never had a divine encounter with Him in which their lives were dramatically changed. Sometimes it takes a tragedy for people to receive a revelation of Jesus. They love God and most of them are born again. They have their "birthright," but they do not have the *blessing beyond the birthright* that Jacob received.

At the passing of King Uzziah, Isaiah in his grief "saw the Lord," repented of his own sins (v. 5), received forgiveness and cleansing (v. 7), heard a new call for his life, and surrendered to follow it (v. 8). Isaiah's response must have been influenced by the scene he saw in heaven with the seraphs ("burning ones") worshipping God. That scene must have been awesome!

Notice the posture of these celestial beings who evidently remain constantly in the "presence of the Lord":

•With two wings, they covered their faces — that represents reverence for the holiness of God.

•With two wings, they covered their feet — that represented humility before the presence of God.

•With two wings, they were flying — that represents service to God — and as they flew, they proclaimed the holiness of the Lord.

The holiness of God finds its most articulate expression in the condemnation of sin. When you have a divine encounter with a Holy God — coming face to face with Him — you cannot go away unchanged. For too long now, we have sought His hand and not His face. His hand is His help, but His face is His character, and His character is holy.

May we once again *see the face of God* which changes our unregenerate natures and sanctifies our lives to Jesus Christ. Amen!

13

Coming in on Broken Pieces

The rest were to get there on planks or on pieces of the ship. In this way everyone reached land in safety.

Acts 27:44

Several times in this book, I have mentioned brokenness and restructuring. During this shaking of the Church, the attacks of the devil, and during the coming storm of the shaking of the whole world, we need to learn something from Paul's voyage to Rome.

When Paul and those with him — which included Luke — and the other prisoners bound for Rome embarked with the centurian in charge of them, it was already late in the season. They were taking a chance in starting out on the Mediterranean Sea so late. The winter season of storms was just beginning.

Paul warned them that the voyage would be dangerous and would bring great loss to the ship and its cargo and to their own lives. But the centurian would not listen, and *the majority* decided what was to be done. Not God, not even the man of God, but *the majority* decided. (That was their first mistake.)

When they started out, there was a gentle breeze, and all of them — except Paul and his followers — **thought they had obtained what they wanted** (Acts 27:13). But before long, a "northeaster," a wind of hurricane force, blew down on them.

The shaking is just about over; however, things may get worse before they get better. God is still purging and purifying His people. Perhaps there will be more disaster, but if you decide now not to jump ship, you will make the shore — even if you have to come in on a piece of a broken dream.

As I have already pointed out, we are going through a transition. We are crossing the threshing floor. We are changing camps. There is a changing of the guard. God is doing something new. I call this time a divine crossroads or intersection in the history of the Church. We may get dirty and dusty. We may fall, stumble, and blunder, but we are still the Church of Jesus Christ, that little cloud on the horizon that Elijah's servant saw, and God has everything under control.

Watch Out for Over-Confidence

First there is a voyage, which starts out with a gentle breeze, then a storm blows up. When a storm comes up in your life, in your ministry, in your marriage, what do you do? A storm does not necessarily mean shipwreck, but sometimes it does, so we need to be careful. Mistaking a premature calmness for the peace of God can be dangerous. That is the danger of over-confidence.

Never stop listening for that still, small voice, and never stop being sober, vigilant, and alert. The Bible says that if you think you are strong, to watch yourself. Some of you are pointing fingers at others who have failed. Paul warned that when we think we are strong is the time to beware of a fall.

> So, if you think you are standing firm, be careful that you don't fall!
>
> 1 Corinthians 10:12

Before long, the ship was caught by the storm and not able to head into the wind. I have seen many ministries, churches, and Christians caught in the storm so they can barely head into the wind. Luke writes that: **We gave way to it and were driven along** (Acts 27:15b). I find people caught in a storm are the same way today. They are driven along from one day to the next, almost directionlessly. The winds are blowing, the lightning is flashing, the thunder is rolling, the waves are splashing over into the boat — and they are sitting there being driven along. They are so locked into the storm they do not know what to do. They have lost their sense of direction. Their spiritual vision is blurred. But God is stronger than our storms.

> For God did not give us a spirit of timidity (fear), but a spirit of power, of love and of self-discipline.
>
> 2 Timothy 1:7

God did not give us a spirit of timidity or fear, but a spirit of power in the midst of a storm, and a spirit of love, a sound mind, and self-discipline in the middle of a storm. You do not have to lose your senses. You do not have to have a nervous breakdown or lose your place in God.

> The ship was caught by the storm and could not head into the wind; so we gave way to it and were driven along. As we passed to the lee of a small island called Cauda, *we were hardly able to make the lifeboat secure.* When the men had hoisted it aboard, they passed ropes under the

> ship itself to hold it together. **Fearing that they**
> **would run aground on the sandbars of Syrtis, they**
> **lowered the sea anchor and** *let the ship be driven*
> *along.*
>
> **Acts 27:15-17**

Even the emergency back-up system (the lifeboat) seemed to be in jeopardy. Sometimes we have to lower the anchor and let go. We need to stop worrying. There are times when a computer will not work, when the mailing list will not work, when the fund-raising program will not work. Then you have to let go, allow yourself to be driven along, and place it all in the Lord's hands.

I used to hear Oral Roberts say, "We *cannot* do it without Him, and He *will not* do it without us."

We have to decide not to **be anxious about anything, but in everything, by prayer and petition, with thanksgiving, present your requests to God** (Phil. 4:6). When you have worked as hard as you can to get someone in your family saved — perhaps even crammed Jesus down their throats — you have to leave that person's salvation up to God. You have done all that you can do, sometimes even more than you should have.

Some people believe Christians are never supposed to go through anything. Our lives are supposed to always be "goody, goody, goody," and "happy, happy, happy." Those people do not know what they are talking about. Paul advised Timothy:

> ...**Everyone who wants to live a godly life**
> **in Christ Jesus will be persecuted, while evil men**
> **and impostors will go from bad to worse,**
> **deceiving and being deceived.**
>
> **2 Timothy 3:12**

But Paul added a "postscript" to that thought when he wrote to the church at Rome:

> **I consider that our present sufferings are not worth comparing with the glory that will be revealed in us.**
>
> **Romans 8:18**

Glory Is on the Way

We have not seen anything yet. We are going to win this thing. There is always hope in the Lord.

> **We took such a violent battering from the storm that the next day they began to throw the cargo overboard. On the third day, they threw the ship's tackle overboard with their own hands.**
>
> **Acts 27:18,19**

Notice how they reacted ... **the cargo** — "the message." We are taking a battering in the Church right now. There are some people who want to throw the message overboard, because the ship is being battered. They are uptight. They think the Bible does not work, because it does not seem to be working for those who are preaching it.

Even some Christians are saying, "They are all a bunch of frauds. They are all liars. It will not work."

Whether I make it or not, the Bible is right. An old song we used to sing when I was a boy was not proper English, but it was truth:

> God is God, and God don't never change. God is God, and He'll always be the same. He is God in Oklahoma, and He is God in Tennessee. He is God all over the universe, and He is God inside of me!

The Word says He is the same yesterday, today, and forever. (Heb. 13:8.) I do not care what the devil says, or what people say: We are still the Body of Christ, and we are going to come through this storm. Now is not the time to jump ship.

The people on board Paul's ship threw the cargo overboard. They said, "It's not working." On the third day, they threw over the *tackle*. That is the equipment, the gifts, the instruments, the tools of evangelism. Some have quit praising and quit having worship music. They have lost their burden for souls. Luke wrote that they threw the tackle overboard **with their own hands** — by the work of the flesh.

Some people are saying, "Let's just go to church and sing one or two little songs. Let's not bother to stay long, because it is time to mourn. The media say we are not going to make it."

The media spokespeople do not predict our future! They may think they know what is going on in the world, but they do not know the Bible. Let's not throw out the gifts of the Spirit. Do not treat prophecy with contempt. Only the carnal will discard the "tackle." No storm can be so bad that the instruments, gifts, and tools of our spiritual trade become unnecessary.

Storms May Come
Even When We Are in the Will of God

Also, we need to remember that a storm can come even when we are in the will of God, not just when we are missing God. Remember that the disciples were in a boat crossing to the other shore of the Sea of Galilee *which Jesus had told them to do*, and a storm came up. Were they being disobedient or out of His will? No, they were being obedient, but the storm came up anyway.

Because a storm comes up does not mean you are not where God wants you to be. The storms of life can be used by God to test your faith. Sometimes the highest quality of faith begins with fear. Fear is the opposite of faith, but not necessarily the absence of it.

Billy Sunday said, "When fear knocked on my door, faith answered, and there wasn't anybody there."

As the disciples began to cross the sea of Galilee:

> **Without warning, a furious storm came up**
> **on the lake, so that the waves swept over the boat.**
> **Matthew 8:24**

Mark and Luke both wrote about a similar incident. (Mark 4:35-41; Luke 8:22-26.) They said a squall came down on the lake, and the disciples' boat was in great danger of being swamped. The men woke up Jesus for He was sleeping in the back of the boat. First, He rebuked them for lack of faith, *then* He rebuked the wind and the waves. To the disciples, He said, "Peace," and to the storm, He said, "Be still!"

If you are in the will of God, and you know it, and you know that Jesus is in your boat, why are you concerned when a storm blows up? Jesus is the only One Who can take us through the storms of life.

Don't Give Up Hope

When neither sun nor stars appeared for

**many days and the storm continued raging, we
finally gave up all hope of being saved.**

Acts 27:20

In recent weeks and months, many people have
said, "I have given up hope, because I thought this
thing was over, and a year later, it hit us again. I am
giving up all hope of being saved. We are going
under. We are not going to make it. I am going to stop
going to church. I will never send another dollar to
another ministry."

Those are deadly, negative emotions born out of
a lack of faith and a fear of the storm. The news
media say to study a ministry and know where every
dollar goes before you contribute. So suddenly we
have all become private investigators, snooping
around like dogs sniffing a hot trail.

People who would not even tithe before are
now saying, "What is the preacher doing with the
money?"

Don't become a private investigator and go
around looking for dirt all the time. Men make
mistakes. Churches and ministries are shaken and
sometimes fall. But God is still God! Never let your
faith waver. Never give up all hope of being saved
out of your troubles. It is all right to make sure you
believe in the ministry to which you give, but also
you must make sure your heart is pure *when* you
give. God will know your heart, even if the ministry
or church to which you give falls or fails in some way.
Again, never give up hope.

**After the men had gone a long time without
food, Paul stood up before them and said: "Men,
you should have taken my advice not to sail from**

**Crete; then you would have spared yourselves this
damage and loss.**

Acts 27:21

Everybody is not going to have a church like Dr.
Paul Yonggi Cho's in Seoul, Korea, with more than a
half million members. We thank God for that, and He
may do that in a few other places — but that is not
God's vision for every pastor. If you have three
hundred people, do not feel you need three thousand.
Seek God to see if you have all He wants you to have.
Competing with other ministers is giving pastors
heart attacks and ulcers. *No one can beat you at being
you.* Do not compete with anyone else. Serve your
own ministry and your own community as God
directs you.

God is saying to us what Paul said to the ship's
captain and crew: "You should have taken My advice
not to sail from Crete, then you would have spared
yourselves this damage and loss." (Acts 27:21.)

Some Christians are getting in trouble because
they "bit off something too big to chew." We are
enlarging our church in Tulsa, but it is because our
present facility is too small and this is what God said
for us to do. We are not building because the pastor
down the street or across town is building. Don't "sail
from Crete" until God says "Sail," and you will save
yourself unnecessary grief.

Paul urged them to keep up their courage
because only the ship would be lost. In the beginning,
he had a witness from the Lord which made him
think that all would be lost, but after much fasting
and prayer, an angel brought him a message of hope
from God:

> Last night an angel of the God whose I am
> and whom I serve stood beside me and said, 'Do
> not be afraid, Paul. You must stand trial before
> Caesar; and God has graciously given you the lives
> of all who sail with you.' So keep up your courage,
> men, for I have faith in God that it will happen
> just as he told me.
>
> **Acts 27:23,24**

Paul said not a person would be lost, only the ship. Let "the ship" go. The ministry may be destroyed, but you do not have to go down with it. If I heard from God that I had to give up my church or my ministry, I would let it go. If I held onto anything after God said it was being destroyed, I would get bitter, angry, upset, and frustrated. I might even backslide from my calling and decide to go sell insurance instead of preach.

We must stand trial before Caesar. The world system is going to try us. The media, the American Civil Liberties Union, the IRS, the Supreme Court will try us, and there will be some destruction. They are going to point the finger at us, *but God has graciously given us the lives of all who sail with us.* (Acts 27:24.)

If you decide to jump ship and not stand and support the Church, if you decide not to believe God, not to attend church, and not to love and serve Him, you are going to be drowned.

Let me tell you something, Caesar (systems of the world): We are coming in even if it is on broken pieces of ministry, we are coming ashore in safety! We may be down, but don't count us out. We may come in on "pieces or fragments of timber" — ministries, dreams, visions, plans, or even broken hearts — but we will float onto the shore of a new beginning and a new day in Jesus Christ.

14

Take Another Scroll

It has been said that experience is not only what happens to you, it is what you do *with* what happens to you.

Some time ago, I was holding a meeting in Nassau, The Bahamas, when right in the middle of the worship service, I became uncomfortable and too warm. So I went back up to my room for a few minutes and sat on the balcony. For some reason, I could not get into the service, although I had to preach that night.

Sitting on that fourth floor balcony overlooking the ocean and gazing out at the tranquil and beautiful scene, I began to look back over the year. I reflected on the things that had happened in my ministry, and on what my church, Higher Dimensions in Tulsa, Oklahoma, and the ministry had gone through. It was one of the most difficult years we had ever experienced but also one of the most productive. My church and ministry were able to carry out our goal of emphasizing evangelism and the spreading of the Gospel around the world.

Finances have been good, and we acquired a building for the church, but I have lost some dear friends. I have sustained some personal hurts and wounds.

There were times when I wondered, "God, why are You allowing things to happen as they have happened? What is wrong? What do I do? I am doing the best I know how, preaching the best I know how, praying and teaching the people to pray and to fast, to become consecrated, and to totally surrender their lives."

As I sat on that balcony, with hot, salty tears rolling down my cheeks, I sort of "licked my wounds" in a private moment of melancholy. I was just minutes away from preaching, but God was ministering to me.

I thought, "Lord, this place right here hurts. I want you to know that hurts. And there is a hurt over here. Would you touch me here? Would you heal me in my spirit, my mind, and my emotions? Lord, inspire my faith, encourage my heart. I don't know what's happening. I am not sure of things."

I realized that in the days to come, there were going to be a lot of times when many of us were not going to be sure what was happening. We were not going to understand. But one thing I began to see we must do gracefully is *dare to not understand.* Another thing we must learn to do is *dare to be misunderstood.*

The thing that became clear to me in those few moments on the balcony was that I had enlisted in a war, and there are casualties in every war. But whenever I lose a battle or a rebellious king burns up my book as one did for the prophet Jeremiah, I will pick up another scroll and write it again.

A wise man once said, "Better to fail at something that will ultimately succeed than to succeed at something that will ultimately fail."

Write It Again

I was so happy during my college years at Oral Roberts University when my biology professor allowed those who did not pass to take the exam again. I had a full schedule. I was active with the ORU World Action Singers and the Souls A'Fire Choir, preached and traveled here and there, and maintained other extracurricular activities. There was not as much time to spend on my studies as there should have been. But every time I flunked a test, the biology teacher allowed me to take it again — and then I passed.

The words God told Jeremiah to write involved twenty-three years of prophetic utterance. How he remembered them, I do not know, unless he kept notes or God harbored them in his spirit.

> **In the fourth year of Jehoiakim son of Josiah king of Judah, this word came to Jeremiah from the Lord: "Take a scroll and write on it all the words I have spoken to you concerning Israel, Judah and all the other nations from the time I began speaking to you in the reign of Josiah till now. Perhaps when the people of Judah hear about every disaster I plan to inflict on them, each of them will turn from his wicked way; then I will forgive their wickedness and their sin."**
>
> **Jeremiah 36:1-3**

God's Objective Is Repentance

Remember, God's objective was to *forgive* their wickedness and sin. He did not want to chide them. He did not want to punish them. He does not like demonstrating His wrath. His objective in a warning prophecy is to get people to repent.

> So Jeremiah called Baruch son of Neriah,
> and while Jeremiah dictated all the words the Lord
> had spoken to him, Baruch wrote them on the
> scroll.
>
> Jeremiah 36:4

Now skip over to the 21st and 22nd verses:

> The king sent Jehudi to get the scroll, and
> Jehudi brought it from the room of Elishama the
> secretary and read it to the king and all the
> officials standing beside him. It was the ninth
> month and the king was sitting in the winter
> apartment, with a fire burning in the firepot in
> front of him.

I want you to picture this proud king. He was probably reclining, warming his toes by the fire. It was wintertime. He had not permitted Jeremiah to speak out loud because his prophecies were "negative." The king was relaxing, and Jeremiah's prophecies got on his nerves.

Jeremiah kept saying, "You folks are going down if you don't change your ways," and they did not want to change their ways. They did not want to repent.

The king had said, "All right, Jeremiah, you are no longer even allowed to come near the temple area," because the prophet had given a discourse there that had really stirred the people.

If you preach the Word as it is supposed to be preached, you either make folks shouting and glad, or fighting mad. But there *will* be a response! I like to say that I preach to comfort the afflicted and to afflict the comfortable.

Because the king had told Jeremiah not to speak publicly, God said:

"All right, Jeremiah. The king wants war. He won't let you speak it verbally, so write it, and then you stay away from the temple, but send some of the brethren to read it."

So his men went and read it in the temple, and the king's officials heard it. They took it to the king to get his response. The king's response is recorded in the book of Jeremiah:

> Whenever Jehudi had read three or four columns of the scroll, the king cut them off with a scribe's knife and threw them into the firepot, until the entire scroll was burned in the fire.
>
> Jeremiah 36:23

The king would say, "Read it," and the official would read a few columns. Then the king would take out his knife and say, "Bring it here, and just cut it off. Toss it into the fire. Who does that prophet think he is? All right, read some more."

The secretary would read some more, and the king would cut off some more of the scroll and throw it into the fire. He continued to do that until he had destroyed the entire scroll. (Jer. 36:24-32.)

Of the Old Testament prophets, probably Jeremiah had the most thankless task of all. He was called from his childhood, and his ministry spanned some forty years. He lived to see his prophecies fulfilled. Sometimes he is called "the weeping prophet." He also wrote the book of Lamentations. His ministry was one of lamentation because his message was one of grief over the sins of Judah.

No preacher enjoys having his message ignored, but neither does he really like to deliver the kind of message and do the kinds of things Jeremiah was called to do. But I learned from Jeremiah that God sometimes allows the devil to do things — such as burn up one of His prophetic messages or destroy some great work he called you to build or establish— and at the time we may not understand why. God seems much too big and too powerful to allow His Word to be destroyed. However, in this instance, God allowed the king to burn up the prophecy that must have taken Jeremiah and Baruch at least a year of laborious work to get down on a scroll. They had to write it all by hand.

Lives Also Need To Be "Rewritten"

Many of our lives are like Jeremiah's ministry. Terrible, disastrous things come: A marriage is broken, a family is shattered, a business is lost, a ministry decreases. You flunk out of school. You do something wrong. Everything goes haywire. Then what do you do? You don't give up, and you don't give in. You do as Jeremiah did: You start all over again, pick up the scroll, and rewrite the story.

> **After the king burned the scroll containing the words that Baruch had written at Jeremiah's dictation, the word of the LORD came to Jeremiah: "Take another scroll and write on it all the words that were on the first scroll, which Jehoiakim king of Judah burned up."**
>
> **Jeremiah 36:28,29**

There are going to be times when things that are dear to you may be destroyed, and when the devil will play mind games on you. I have seen people all over this country go through it.

Ministries and ministers right now are being sued. There are all kinds of contentions. I have heard many great preachers talk about some of the painful things they have been going through in their own ministries and lives. Their families were rising up against them, and some of these preachers were weeping. They were going through such difficult times, and they were wondering why God was allowing those who were against them to succeed.

Have you ever felt the Lord let the bad man get by? Have you ever lived across the street from an atheist or some big sinner whose house was three times bigger than yours? All of his children were doing well and his cars were perfect. You lived across the street with "Praise the Lord" on your door, and your washing machine was broken, your heating system broke down, creditors were knocking on your door — or perhaps you had a "Honk-if-you-love-Jesus" sticker on your car as you accidentally rammed it into a telephone pole!

Your house burned up, and the atheist across the street said, "I wonder why the Christian over there is going through so much hell?"

However, if you never meet the devil head on, it is a good sign you are walking with him, because the only way for you to meet him head on is for both of you to be going in opposite directions. If you are walking with God, you will meet the devil head-on sometimes. When you do, he may knock you back a little bit, but surely goodness and mercy shall follow you. (Ps. 23:6.)

I am so glad that goodness and mercy are behind me, because every time I get knocked back, the devil can only push me so far before I bump into goodness and mercy following me all the days of my life!

I would like to have a prophetic ministry, but I am not sure that I want one quite like Jeremiah's. Many preachers also have the nightmare that perhaps their ministries will someday be like Noah's, who preached one hundred and twenty years and did not get anyone saved but his family. Paul said to **endure hardship with us like a good soldier** (2 Tim. 2:3).

Jeremiah wanted to obey the Lord. He was telling Judah, "You obey the Lord, and things will be different." But Jeremiah obeyed the Lord and was hated by mankind!

Perhaps you have done the best you could in your marriage and your home, or maybe you stumbled a bit somewhere. However, in your business or your ministry, you are struggling to do what is right. Then it seems the enemy slips in, and God allows the devil to do something terrible. Or have you ever really studied for a test as best you knew how, and then did not do well on it?

Life can be filled with all kinds of unpleasant and frustrating experiences. We need to be aware of them and not be defeated by them.

Jeremiah, with his thankless task as a prophet, must have been quite a little annoyed by many of the things that happened to him. He actually got mad at times and said things like, **Drag them off like sheep to be butchered! Set them apart for the day of slaughter!** (Jer. 12:3.)

Then God said to him, "If you have gotten worn out racing with men, how are you going to run against horses? If you stumble while you are just walking on level ground, what will you do in the thickets?" (Jer. 12:5.)

I believe God is preparing the Church to go through a baptism of fire. I think He is getting us ready to endure hardships such as we have never seen before. However, these times will be accompanied by great miracles and demonstrations of His power. We will need great miracles and great manifestations in order to keep our courage through these painful tests and trials.

God is saying to us, "If you are not making it now in these comparatively secure and prosperous times, how will you make it in the hard times?"

"They Said ...."

> They said, "Come, let's make plans against Jeremiah; for the teaching of the law by the priest will not be lost, nor will counsel from the wise, nor the word from the prophets. So come, let's attack him with our tongues and pay no attention to anything he says."
>
> **Jeremiah 18:18**

How many times have you been attacked by a tongue? As a good Christian, walking in love, you cannot physically slap someone — though there may be times when you are tempted! But that tongue, that tongue! You can attack or be attached with a tongue. You must learn how to deal with those things. Learn how to simply "write it again" without tearing at yourself and someone else, without fighting and without getting vindictive.

Jeremiah had a task more thankless than any of ours. Some renegade citizens of Judah refused to go into the God-ordained exile and forced him to go to Egypt with them, and that is the last he is recorded in Scripture. We do not even know for certain how he died. By the 20th chapter of Jeremiah, you can tell he is very upset.

> O Lord, you deceived me, and I was deceived; you overpowered me and prevailed. I am ridiculed all day long; everyone mocks me.
>
> Whenever I speak, I cry out proclaiming violence and destruction. So the word of the Lord has brought me insult and reproach all day long.
>
> But if I say, "I will not mention him or speak any more in his name," his word is in my heart like a burning fire, shut up in my bones. I am weary of holding it in; indeed, I cannot.
>
> **Jeremiah 20:7-9**

In other words, Jeremiah was saying, "Lord, I am between 'a rock and a hard place.' Sometimes I do not want to prophesy to them, because they are not listening to me, and they are laughing and mocking me. Yet, there is a drive on the inside that makes me keep on writing it again."

The devil is nothing but a bluff. You must take the authority that is in you as one whose body is a temple of the Holy Spirit, look the devil square in the eye, flex your muscles of faith, show him your "dukes," and tell him you mean business. Get up off your knees and emerge from the chambers of consecration, and tell the devil that **the one who is in you is greater than the one who is in the world** (1 John 4:4).

Take another scroll, and write it again because the greatest things are yet to come.

15
"The Greatest Things Are Yet To Come"

In November of 1975, I had the privilege of appearing as a guest on the "I Believe in Miracles" telecast hosted by the late Kathryn Kuhlman. That was the last series of taped telecasts that she was able to do before she went home to be with the Lord three and a half months later.

I saw Ms. Kuhlman in person for the first time in about 1967 when my family attended one of her monthly miracle services at the famous Shrine Auditorium in Los Angeles. I was just a teenager, but she made an indelible impression on my mind.

In the spring of 1972, I met her personally. It was the close of my freshman year at Oral Roberts University, and she was the baccalaureate speaker for that year's graduating class. We hit it off immediately and seemed to enjoy what I felt was a mutual admiration for each other that continued until her death in February 1976.

I had raced across the campus that warm sun-splashed day, pushing my way through graduates bubbling over with accomplishment in front of their proud families, in order to get to the cool Fireside Lounge on the first floor of the Student Union Building where a special reception was being held for Ms. Kuhlman. The reception was by "invitation only," but I was determined to meet her. I felt almost divinely called to do so.

Recently, I had been chosen as one of the ORU World Action Singers, and I was to begin appearing weekly on the nationally televised "Oral Roberts and You" program. At that time, his program was number one in Christian television programming. So I was prepared to use whatever clout (if any) my new position entailed, if anyone attempted to question my presence at the reception. However, that never became necessary.

When I walked in, she acted as if she was expecting me.

She smiled, and I ran up to her and said, "Oh, Miss Kuhlman, may I hug you?"

She said, "Oh, God love you," and I just sort of melted, and she began to prophesy to me. Then she said, "You know, we're friends, don't you?"

"Yes, Ma'am," I said.

"We're family. You know that, don't you?"

"Yes, Ma'am."

She said, "You're marked, young man. When you're in Los Angeles, you must come and see me. You must come to the telecast."

In 1975, when I flew out to be on the show, none of us realized how soon she would be gone, although I had begun to get an intimation of her death months before. That day in Los Angeles, some physical things connected with her enlarged heart had become obvious. She seemed so frail, and she looked gaunt that cool Tuesday morning as we disembarked from our separate cars in front of the CBS studios.

Usually when I saw her, I would run up and kiss and hug her, and she would kiss and hug me, and we would hold on to each other. But that morning, I was stunned by the cold, chilly death that I saw. I cannot explain to you what I mean, but I withdrew somewhat. I went over as usual, but I did not kiss her.

In spite of seeming weak and feeble, she was her usual warm and effervescent self, the way she had always been whenever we had met — which had not been very often. However, each encounter had been special and made a significant impression on me.

That morning, I greeted Loush, her personal driver of twenty-five years, who had been miraculously healed in one of her meetings many years earlier, and said hello to Tink and Sue Wilkerson, personal friends of mine who were acting as voluntary assistants to Ms. Kuhlman. When I turned to Kathryn, she extended a long, frail-looking arm toward me, locked her arms with mine, and pulled me with surprising strength away from the rest of the small entourage. We walked slowly but deliberately down the long narrow corridor to her private dressing room.

Only a few weeks earlier, I had opened my post office box on the ORU campus to find a personal letter from her. The last paragraph of that letter I will never forget. The impact remains with me to this very day. Here is what she wrote:

> How vast a trust is our earthly life, and its twelve brief hours shall soon be gone. May we diligently strive to fill each day with our best service for God so that our works will live on beyond the day our voices are hushed with the last silence.

As a twenty-two-year-old aspiring evangelist, I was moved formidably by her words and felt even then that they were a hint of her imminent departure from this world. Earlier, I had sensed in my spirit that she would not be with us too much longer and had written for permission to appear on her telecast to share my personal testimony. Also, I wanted to spend what I knew would be precious moments with her as often as possible.

In retrospect, my action seems a bit presumptuous, but at that time, I was sure it was something God wanted me to do. Apparently Kathryn felt the same. Shortly after that last letter from her, Tink Wilkerson phoned me in my dormitory room at ORU to tell me there had been a guest cancellation for the telecast, and Kathryn wanted me to fly out the next week to fill the vacancy.

My entire last meeting with Kathryn Kuhlman was all in God's special and sovereign design. Because of it, I have not been the same person.

One of the last things she said to me was, "I want to live. I want to live more than I ever have before in my life."

I asked why, and she said, "These are the greatest hours the church has ever known, *but I believe the greatest days of all are yet to come.*"

She repeatedly spoke of a divine visitation she believed was soon to come to the Church. She spoke as if she could see it with her spiritual eyes, staring off into space as if she were viewing a television screen in another world or in some distant dimension. With a look of exaltation on her face and the misty sheen of tears in her eyes, she said it again, "I want to live. I want to see it. I want to be a part of it."

She looked at me, and said, "Don't you see it, Carlton? Can't you feel it coming?"

Then, pointing a long, narrow, and perfectly manicured finger at me, she said, "You'll see it, Carlton. You'll be right in the big middle of it, and when you are, you will remember that Kathryn Kuhlman told you it would be so."

Then she prayed this prayer:

> Bless him, wonderful Jesus, just bless him. And one of these days, when he has lived his last day and preached his last sermon, I pray that thousands and thousands will enter the gates of glory because of Carlton Pearson. I pray but one (more) thing, God, give him the best that You have. You giveth the Holy Spirit without measure. Give to Carlton the best that You have.

> Oh, dear Jesus, bless him, just bless him with a divine blessing. Bless this young life that is being shaped and molded underneath those everlasting arms. Overshadow him with Your love, and mold him. Give him, I pray, divine love, wisdom, and understanding. Use him to shake the world spiritually for You!

When she finally died on a stormy Friday night in Tulsa, I was told the next morning that she was gone. On the Sunday following her death, I saw the very television show that we had taped that day in Los Angeles three and a half months earlier. The night before she died, I dreamed that I saw her behind a baseball diamond. They drove her up in a long, white limousine, and she got out and walked over to the fence. I rushed over to where she was and kissed her through the fence. I felt somehow, through the dream that I had said goodby to one of the greatest spiritual leaders of the 20th century.

As we approach the year 2000 and enter the 21st century, we are more than likely facing the last century before the Second Coming of Jesus. I do not believe the 21st century will go even to the halfway mark before Jesus returns to earth. In the meantime, the greatest revival and the greatest visitation of God that the world has ever known will take place. A lot must transpire in the hearts of men before this revival can fully come, but I believe with Kathryn Kuhlman: "The greatest days are yet to come."

We tend to forget that God is omniscient. He already knew this shaking was coming, and He knows how it will turn out. The Church must *trust* as well as obey.

There Is No Crisis in Heaven

Two weeks before Easter, 1988, I was sitting in my house preparing a message to deliver on fearful disciples who hid themselves in the Upper Room after the Resurrection. The disciples and followers of Jesus had shut the doors and locked the windows, hiding from the Jews, because they were afraid that what happened to Jesus would happen to them. It was a time of crisis in their lives and in their ministries.

I was crying as I read the account in Acts 2, and I said, "Lord, sometimes I feel like running into some room, shutting the door, and saying, 'Lord, I don't want to preach. I don't want to pray. I don't want to grow. I don't want to do anything." The ministry at times can be hard, and a minister can experience deep feelings of despair, grief, and disillusionment.

The higher you go in popularity, the harder it is. When no one knows who you are, you are not going to be shot at, but the higher you go in success and visibility, the easier a target you are and the heavier the weapons used against you.

I said, "Lord, these men right at the top are easy targets. The enemy is not only taking pot shots, he is actually shooting some of them and knocking them off the ladder. I am not sure about all of this, Lord!"

One internationally known evangelist shared with me not long ago that in 1980, the Lord told him to get out of the media completely, to get off television. He realizes now that anyone who is visible is a target. God had to have some leaders who were not so visible.

Sitting there reading my pre-Easter message, I began to think about what the Church was going to do, and then with my spiritual eyes, I saw Jesus sitting in a chair across from me with His legs casually crossed. It was like a vision or a dream, but I was completely awake.

He leaned over toward me and said, "There is no crisis in heaven."

I said, "What do You mean, Lord? The voices of Your top spokesmen have been silenced. Prostitutes are making sport at the Church's expense. The media is lambasting us. There are very few miracles. There are not many visions, and the Word of the Lord is rare. How can you say, 'There is no crisis in heaven'?"

Jesus said, "*We* have everything under control."

And then I saw something almost unbelievable. I looked over at my dining room table, and again with my spiritual eyes, I saw four angels sitting there. They were talking very quietly, and I could not hear what they were saying. But they were smiling, laughing, bantering back and forth. They were so relaxed and seemed so serene and so tranquil.

Then immediately behind me in the living room area, there were about half a dozen of them watching television. I don't know what they were watching, whether it was a religious channel or CNN News, but they too were very relaxed and casual.

And I could not see it all, but I felt that in my kitchen, someone was fixing a bowl of my favorite cereal. Back in the utility room, I have a washer and dryer, and I heard them running. I thought some angels might have been washing their robes or something. I know it sounds odd, but for a few minutes, my entire house was filled with the glory of heaven with angels all over the place.

The Holy Spirit ministered to me then, saying, "They know exactly what is going on. They are so calm because they know. It is time for this transition to take place. The old prophets are going up, but their mantles are coming down."

He said, "Stop mourning. Get out of that room. Unlock the doors. Unlock the windows. Do not worry about being shot at by the world. Just live holy. Live right, and go forth in the name of the Lord."

We are going to have to kiss the past goodby. It is gone. What God did in the past is gone. The ministries that are shaking have had their day, most of them. Many of the leaders of the last move of God have done what they were called to do. Many of them will go home to God, and others will not have the same influence they once had. They were yesterday's "parents," the fathers of the last generation. We must kiss them goodby.

God Has Something New To Do

We have to give up the past. We have mourned because we did not know what God was doing. I am tired of mourning. I am tired of walking around sad because of all the things that have happened.

I am saying, "Lord, okay, we are going to have to bury that and go on."

The Lord once scolded the prophet Samuel for mourning the past after He had rejected it. Samuel was mourning for Saul, and God said:

> ..."How long will you mourn for Saul, since I have rejected him as king over Israel? Fill your horn with oil and be on your way; I am sending you to Jesse of Bethlehem. I have chosen one of his sons to be king."
>
> 1 Samuel 16:1

God has something new in mind. Just as Elisha did, we have to burn up the plow and destroy the

201

oxen of the past and follow the leadership of the Holy Spirit.

In spite of the things that have happened in the past two years, God is still God, Jesus is still on the throne, and the Holy Spirit is still with us. The Church is still here. God's miracle-working power will still be with us if we handle the anointing properly. It does not matter what the media says, or who goes on or off television. If God wants us on, then we will be on; if not, we will not be. However, we know He wants the world to hear the Gospel.

Today, the Holy Spirit is saying, "Get your horn filled with a new anointing. Get the new oil, and go on about your business in the name of the Lord."

That does not mean we are to be calloused and insensitive to things that have happened of late. Our hearts are broken. We have wept, fasted, and prayed, but at the same time, we cannot stay around the grave as Mary Magdalene did looking for something that has been resurrected. We cannot stay too busy looking in the grave to see that the Man in it has come out and is alive and well, standing behind us.

Seven Things About the Harvest

I believe Jesus is standing behind us saying:

"Okay, I am through with that. I know where those men of the old guard are. Stop looking at the grave, turn around and look at me. I am in charge of everything. Get on with your work."

There are seven points I want to make about the coming harvest:

1) The first thing that happens when the harvest comes in is rain. After the rain, then 2) they cut the grain. That is part of the revival. 3) The third thing they did was gather it, and 4) then they bound the grain together in sheaves. He cuts us down, then binds us all together, and ties us up in Himself.

After the grain was cut, gathered, bound, and united, it was 5) threshed, flailed or treaded. God is threshing us to shake away the chaff. The next thing they did 6) was to sift the grain, to run it through a sieve. Finally, 7) they collected it into the barns, which in our analogy, means churches.

In today's churches, however, we are skipping over points one through six and harvesting the grain right into the barn. It has not rained, the grain has not been cut down and gathered by the Holy Spirit, it has not been bound, threshed or sifted.

I am so concerned for the babies who are wondering, "What is going on in the Body of Christ?"

I am afraid for them. The preachers are having trouble, the media are coming against us, the money is not coming in, and Christians are getting confused. They do not understand. They are standing on the Word, believing God, and still experiencing hell in their lives.

The Church is responsible for making false altar calls:

"Come to Jesus. He will bless you, restore you, help you, heal you, and make your life wonderful."

That is not the whole truth. Sure He will help us and heal us. There are blessings, *but there is persecution along with them. There are trials and tests. There is a purging and a preparatory thing God also does. Jesus only gave challenges; we give bribes.*

> If anyone teaches false doctrines and does not agree to the sound instruction of our Lord Jesus Christ and to godly teaching, he is conceited and understands nothing. He has an unhealthy interest in controversies and arguments that result in envy, quarreling, malicious talk, evil suspicions, and constant friction between men of corrupt mind, who have been robbed of the truth and who think that godliness is a means to financial gain.
>
> But godliness with contentment is great gain.
>
> 1 Timothy 6:3-6

Sin is sin. God is calling for people who will tell the truth. Money has nothing to do with what God is going to do. His enabling force is not money, but the power of the Holy Spirit. The power of the Holy Spirit is masculine and strong. There is nothing sissy about the Holy Spirit, although His nature is to be as gentle as a dove. Gentleness is not weakness. There is nothing "prissy" about the Holy Spirit. He is the power in the Word, an authority that can command demons, cancers and goiters, and sin to flee in the name of Jesus.

Some Will Despise You

Some people are going to despise you if you follow this call to holiness and allow God to winnow you on His threshing floor. They will see you leaping and dancing before the Lord, and they are going to despise you as Michal did David.

David had been through a great depression during the three months between the death of Uzzah and his learning how to carry the Ark according to God's instructions. He had learned how to carry the Ark, brought it back to Jerusalem in the midst of great rejoicing, given good things to the people, and now has gone home to bless his own household. But what does he find? Contempt in his own wife. The Bible says she despised him, and she did not keep her opinions to herself.

> ...Michal daughter of Saul came out to meet him and said, "How the king of Israel has distinguished himself today, disrobing in the sight of the slave girls, of his servants, as any vulgar fellow would!"
>
> 2 Samuel 6:20

She was jealous, you see. But David was not thinking about the slave girls.

> David said to Michal, "It was before the Lord, who chose me rather than your father or anyone from his house when he appointed me ruler over the Lord's people Israel — I will celebrate before the Lord. I will become even more undignified than this, and I will be humiliated in my own eyes. But by these slave girls you spoke of, I will be held in honor."
>
> And Michal daughter of Saul had no children to the day of her death.
>
> 2 Samuel 6:21-23

David was so happy to have the anointing back that he did not care what anyone thought of him. Let us be that way. Let us act like a chosen generation, learn how to treat the anointing and how to keep it, and rejoice over having it back in the city. We do not need to worry about those who scoff or scorn or look at us with contempt. We are the laborers in the harvest.

We can make it, if we stand up and are bold for the Lord. We can make it, even if we have to float into shore on broken pieces of the ship.

1988: The Year of New Beginnings

I believe something began supernaturally in 1988. Eight is the Biblical number for new beginnings. God is raising up ministries of hope for the Body. In 1977 I had a strange visitation from the Lord. He instructed me: "Remind the saints of the hope."

Eleven years later to the same month, we held a conference sponsored by Higher Dimensions in Tulsa and called it Azusa '88. The theme was "God Can Do It Again."

After that meeting, I had many of those who attended say to me, "Brother, I did not know when I came that I was going to feel this. But I believe I can go home and do it again. I believe now that I can make it."

That is the main purpose for this book: to remind the saints of the hope. God is God, and He is in control. If we understand what is happening and have the vision to see what the prophet saw through the shaking and the attacks of the enemy, we will come out on the other side victorious.

If you have a famine in your life, or if you know God is dealing with some "tares," you need to begin to pray this way:

Heavenly Father, I want to find the fire escape in Jesus. I want to make my way to the other side of the threshing floor in safety. I want to be a part of your endtime church in prayer and humility. I do not want to be up front to be seen. I want to humble myself before You.

If you seek God in all sincerity and humble yourself, you will be prepared and ready to be part of the Church of the Double Portion.

16
The Church of the Double Portion

> "Let me inherit a double portion of your spirit."
>
> 2 Kings 2:9b

When I was a boy growing up in Southern California, one of the favorite times for me was sitting down for the daily family supper. That was the one time when all of us six children were able to sit down with our parents for a time of good food, good family fellowship, and — unless Daddy delivered one of his periodic serious and solemn heart-to-heart lectures — lots of laughter and fun.

My parents were hard-working people, at times working two jobs each to keep food on the table for their six hungry little mouths. It was always a struggle for my folks to get ahead, and an even greater struggle to stay ahead if we ever got there! However, even if some bills were late, we always had a fair amount of food. Seldom was there excess, but nearly always, there was at least enough.

All of us could expect one serving or what we called "a decent helping" of whatever food there was. If any was left over, we were allowed second helpings. Often, we had second portions, but never double helpings on the first serving. We always had enough, but never too much. Double portions were a "no, no." So I grew up with a bias against asking for double portions of anything. Often I have wanted a double portion of a lot of things in life — friends, God, and so forth. But I thought it was unfair and selfish to ask until I began to learn the ways of God and read about Elisha.

I discovered that God usually supplies a surplus. He gives more than enough. Today, I am asking for a double portion of all that has happened prior to this generation. All the miracles, all the power, all the spiritual success, all the finances for ministry — all that God has ever done — *I want a double portion of that for my generation*, for this next wave of God's glory.

Double whatever has happened for the past twenty centuries is what I want for us. This is to be the *Church of the Double Portion.*

I am not discouraged that the last regime is about to leave. Elijah represented the leadership of a particular generation. But when he went, Elisha saw it and knew it. He saw the value of that generation. He knew the anointing that was on Elijah. He saw what God had done through that prophet, and his attitude was this:

"I am going to keep my eyes on you (the last generation) until you depart. I am going to study what you have done. I am going to study everything from you that I can, and then I am going to ask God to give me double what you have and make me double what you were."

I love his attitude.

I have heard all of the things that happened with Bishop Charles Harrison Mason, founder of the

Church of God in Christ, the denomination in which I grew up. I want a double portion of what he had. I have heard of what happened with Billy Sunday, Charles Finney, John Wesley, Martin Luther, Smith Wigglesworth, Oral Roberts, and even the apostles at Pentecost. And I want a double portion of all of that for my generation. I even want a double portion as far back as Elisha and Elijah.

A Double Portion of the Double Portion

Elisha had so much power that even after he had been buried for years, when a dead man was thrown on top of his bones, that person came back to life. (2 Kings 13:21.) Elisha had more of the anointing of God in his dead body than most of us have in our living bodies.

Elisha got a double portion of what Elijah had, and I believe that is what God is going to do for the Church in the 21st century.

Some people think the choice was all Elisha's, but it was not. Elijah chose Elisha first, and then Elisha responded with his faith.

> So Elijah went from there and found Elisha son of Shaphat. He was plowing with twelve yoke of oxen, and he himself was driving the twelfth pair. Elijah went up to him and threw his cloak around him.
>
> Elisha then left his oxen and ran after Elijah. "Let me kiss my father and mother good-by," he said, "and then I will come with you."
>
> 1 Kings 19:19,20

Elisha was using twenty-four oxen when most people had only one or two. It was like a John Deere combine compared to a hoe. The number of oxen Elisha was using shows he was wealthy, and the fact that he was handling twelve yoke of oxen shows he was physically strong.

The cloak, or mantle, represented authority and responsibility. Elijah did not speak to Elisha and say, "Follow me," or anything like that. He did not give him an invitation at all. He simply wrapped his mantle around him and walked off. Elisha, however, after experiencing just a few moments under Elijah's mantle (anointing), immediately left his work as a wealthy farmer and ran after the prophet. He left everything that he had to follow the man of God, to follow that incredible anointing.

Sometimes God does not say anything to you. He simply comes and puts His Spirit on you. That is your cue to respond. Then is the time to give up everything, no matter how much you have.

Notice that Elisha did not say, "Let me go and handle this or take care of that."

He simply said, "Let me kiss my mom and dad goodby."

In other words, he relinquished ties to his nearest and dearest. He was willing to sacrifice both family and future for what he knew was God's will for his life.

> So Elisha left him and went back. He took his yoke of oxen and slaughtered them. He burned the plowing equipment to cook the meat and gave it to the people, and they ate. Then he set out to follow Elijah and became his attendant.
> 1 Kings 19:21

Give Up the Past

It is not covetousness to want a double portion of what Billy Graham has or a double portion of what Oral Roberts and Kenneth Hagin have. They are looking for their successors, because they know the Church will go on after they leave, just as Kathryn Kuhlman prophesied to me.

We must burn up our pasts as Elisha did and set our sights on new horizons. We must totally give up thinking that God is going to do things exactly as He did them in the past. God wants to do something new in the future through us. I am praying for those leaders still with us today. I am praying for every ministry, but I know God has something new to do.

> "You have asked a difficult thing," Elijah said, "yet if you see me when I am taken from you, it will be yours — otherwise not."
>
> As they were walking along and talking together, suddenly a chariot of fire and horses of fire appeared and separated the two of them, and Elijah went up to heaven in a whirlwind. Elisha saw this and cried out, "My father! My father! The chariots and horsemen of Israel!" And Elisha saw him no more. Then he took hold of his own clothes and tore them apart. (This was a sign of mourning, change, and brokenness.)
>
> He picked up the cloak that had fallen from Elijah and went back and stood on the bank of the Jordan. Then he took the cloak that had fallen from him and struck the water with it. "Where now is the Lord, the God of Elijah?" he asked. When he struck the water, it divided to the right and to the left, and he crossed over.
>
> 2 Kings 2:10-14

Immediately, Elisha picked up the mantle of authority. He picked up the anointing and the responsibility and went back to the river.

The first thing this chosen generation must do, as we receive the mantle of the old leaders, is to cross over into another dimension. Cross over into that anointing, that way of thinking, the attitude that now *the authority, the anointing, and the responsibility is on us.*

The Old Ways Are Disappearing

The new leadership must cross over. They must pass the test, only then can they really help the Church. Once the leadership (priests) have crossed over, they can reach back and help the sheep.

> The company of the prophets from Jericho, who were watching, said, "The spirit of Elijah is resting on Elisha." And they went to meet him and bowed to the ground before him. "Look," they said, "we your servants have fifty able men. Let them go and look for your master. Perhaps the Spirit of the Lord has picked him up and set him down on some mountain or in some valley."
>
> 2 Kings 15,16

Notice that the same group of people who had asked Elisha earlier that morning if he knew his master was going to be taken from him (2 Kings 2:5) were the ones who wanted to go look for Elijah after he was taken! It is funny how some people are still looking for the old way, even though they know God is moving, wants to move, or has moved. They are refusing — or at least reluctant — to give it up and move forward in God.

Some of the same people who sense a change and who talk about it in advance are going to be the ones unwilling to accept it when it begins to take place.

They will say, "Are you sure the old way is not still over there somewhere in the bushes or the valleys? Maybe we need to go over there and look for it."

They are still going to be looking for something or even someone who once was used of God. It will be hard for them to believe their denomination, their favorite evangelist, or their favorite teacher or preacher has been removed by God. Some people today do not listen to any messages but those of a certain evangelist who died more than twenty years ago. They sit and listen to cassettes of his past sermons, and they have become a cult. They are as spiritually dead as the man they are mourning is physically dead.

When you attach yourself to that extent to any preacher, teacher, evangelist, prophet, or apostle, you are idolizing that person, and God will judge you. *God is judging those who worship men, and He is judging the men who let people worship them.*

The company of prophets insisted that Elijah should be looked for until Elisha had no choice but to give in and let them mount a search.

> **But they persisted until he was too ashamed to refuse. So he said, "Send them." And they sent fifty men, who searched for three days but did not find him. When they returned to Elisha, who was staying in Jericho, he said to them, "Didn't I tell you not to go?"**
>
> **2 Kings 2:17,18**

Why do people spend three days, three years, or three decades looking for the past? Our God is in motion. He will do a new thing.

The Saints Are Salt and Light

The next thing recorded in 2 Kings involves Elisha's first task after he received the mantle of Elijah.

Some men came to him with a problem: The water in their town was bad. *Water* in the Bible often is representative of the Holy Spirit.

> **The men of the city said to Elisha, "Look, our lord, this town is well situated, as you can see, but the water is bad and the land is unproductive."**
>
> **2 Kings 2:19**

This situation could be referring to many cities in this country today. They are well-situated, but there have been so many speakers, conferences, and groups come through that the Christians in those cities think they have it all. A bad "spirit," one of self-righteousness, pride, and even lethargy has come over those places instead of the sweet, pure, refreshing water of the Holy Spirit.

Even in Tulsa, this is true. Several great leaders live here, many ministries have headquarters here, and many people who do not live here try to come here. The Tulsa area has developed an unproductive spirit. Because of the concentration of ministries here, we should have more fruits and more miracles than anywhere else in the world. Incredible things should be happening here every day. Instead, not any more is happening than in other cities, and sometimes less actually happens. We have slipped into the wrong spirit, the "water" is bad.

So what did Elisha do? He told them to bring him **a new bowl** — a new vehicle, a new instrument, new ideas, a different vessel, a new one (you can't put new wine in old wineskins — Matt. 9:17). He told them to put salt in it — salt purifies and preserves. (2 Kings 2:20.)

We are the salt of the earth, the Bible says (Matt. 5:13), but if salt has lost its savor (its "saltiness"), it is good for nothing but to be thrown out and walked on. The saints of God are salt, and we are light in the darkness of the world.

Today, God is saying, "Get me a new vessel (wineskin) and fill it up with holy people."

> Then he went out to the spring and threw the salt into it, saying, "This is what the Lord says: 'I have healed this water. Never again will it cause death or make the land unproductive.'" And the water has remained wholesome to this day, according to the word Elisha had spoken.
>
> 2 Kings 2:21,22

I believe God is going to purify the spirits of many cities in this coming move. I want to be some of the salt in the new vessel.

My prayer is, "Lord, show me where the new vessel is, and show me how to get into the new container, because I want to bring purity."

Touch Not Mine Anointed

Watch what happened next to the prophet with his new authority.

> **From there Elisha went up to Bethel. As he
> was walking along the road, some youths came out
> of the town and jeered at him. "Go on up, you
> baldhead!" they said. "Go on up, you baldhead!"**
>
> **2 Kings 2:23**

Now Elisha may not have been baldheaded in
the literal sense, for *baldhead* in those days was an
epithet used to humiliate someone. They were calling
him a bad name, taunting him. "Baldhead" also was
a name of derision for someone with leprosy.

> **He turned around, looked at them and
> called down a curse on them in the name of the
> Lord. Then two bears came out of the woods and
> mauled forty-two of the youths. And he went on to
> Mount Carmel and from there returned to
> Samaria.**
>
> **2 Kings 2:24,25**

People will not laugh at those with the
anointing (the Church of the Double Portion) and get
by in this next move of God. There will be immediate
retribution and judgment from God. They may point
their fingers and laugh, but when the new anointing
comes, when the generation of the Church of the
Double Portion begins to move, people will not be
able to make fun as they have in the past.

God will judge them swiftly. Terrible tragedies
will take place. It is wrong to laugh at and scorn
God's people and especially at what the Holy Spirit is
doing through His people. It is a dangerous thing to
fall into the hands of the living God. He said: **Touch
not mine anointed** (Ps. 105:15 KJV). If someone has
God's anointing on them, it will not matter if the
attacker is a representative of the American Civil
Liberties Union or a member of the United States

Supreme Court, or a member of some church somewhere, there will be swift retribution and that by God Himself.

When someone has the anointing of God on them, don't mess with them! Do not talk about them, do not point your finger, do not touch them. If the glory of the Lord is on them, even though you may find something about them that does not look right, just leave it alone. They are God's responsibility. He called them, and He is the only One Who can recall them. We can preach judgment, but we must never pass judgment.

The youths (who could have been up to thirty years of age in those days) made fun of Elisha, and he had no mercy. He turned and cursed them, and bears came and mauled forty-two of them. For the rest of their lives, they carried the scars. The Bible does not say any of them died, even though some may have. All we know is that the bears mauled them, and I am sure they were never the same.

Forty years later, a grandchild may have crawled up on one of those youths' lap and said, "What is that big scar on your face, Grandpa?"

That grandfather would have said, "I got that for making fun of a man of God. Son, never make fun of a man of God. Never mock the Holy Spirit. That is an abomination to God."

The day is coming when God will not tolerate anyone making fun of His men and women, His Church. Galatians 6:7 (KJV) says, **God is not mocked.**

Poison in the Stew

After that, Elisha ran into a situation where there was death in the stew pot. There was a famine, and one of the servants picked the wrong vine or herb, and it poisoned the stew.

> Elisha returned to Gilgal and there was a famine in that region. While the company of the prophets was meeting with him, he said to his servant, "Put on the large pot and cook some stew for these men."
>
> One of them went out into the fields to gather herbs and found a wild vine. He gathered some of its gourds and filled the fold of his cloak. When he returned, he cut them up into the pot of stew, though no one knew what they were. The stew was poured out for the men, but as they began to eat it, they cried out, "O man of God, there is death in the pot!" And they could not eat it.
>
> 2 Kings 4:38-40

The wild vine represents false doctrines, teachings that are poisonous to the Body of Christ. God is going to give us something to change these erroneous doctrines, wild theories, and incredible stories that are not of Him. He also is going to multiply the Word (the food) and feed the people as Jesus when he multiplied the loaves and fishes.

Through worldwide television, radio, and satellites, God is going to multiply the food until the whole world has a chance to be fed. Not all will eat of it, but all will have the chance to eat of it.

In the fifth chapter of 2 Kings, the story is told of how the foreign leader, Naaman, was healed of leprosy. *Foreign leaders and leaders of false doctrines, cults, and religions will be saved.* Wouldn't it be exciting if Gorbechev began speaking in tongues sitting in the Kremlin one day! I actually expect something that incredible to happen in my lifetime. I believe this is the generation of the Church of the Double Portion. The power of God is going to fall on His people again.

In the sixth chapter of 2 Kings, Elisha caused a sunken ax head to float so the prophets could build a bigger house. I believe *we are going to build bigger and larger buildings and enjoy the miraculous intervention of God to do so.*

This is not the time for giving up. It is a time for holding on! Again, I want to point out that the best is yet to come.

17

The 21st Century Church: Bringing Things Back to Life

> But Jehosophat asked, "Is there no prophet of the Lord here, that we may inquire of the Lord through him?"
>
> 2 Kings 3:11

Elijah (a symbol of one generation of spiritual leadership) ran from Jezebel and Ahab, but Elisha (who represents a new generation of leadership) had the heads of state begging for his assistance, his counsel, and his guidance. Government officials will inquire of the Church of the Double Portion for counsel. When the banks fail, when Wall Street is trembling, when major businesses go under, God's Church is still going to be floating above the water, and the world is going to be saying, "What is their secret?"

While the world systems are failing, financially or otherwise, God is going to let His Church be seen rising up like an island in the sea.

The world will be asking, "What is it about those people that enables them to remain successful during a time of recession or depression? Get them in here. Let's find out their secret. Is there any word from the Lord?"

That is going to happen again. They are laughing at us today, but God is going to raise us up. And we will have the last laugh.

Paying the Debts of Other Ministries

In the fourth chapter of Second Kings, we see another interesting situation.

223

> The wife of a man from the company of the prophets cried out to Elisha, "Your servant my husband is dead, and you know that he revered the Lord. But now his creditor is coming to take my two boys as his slaves."
>
> 2 Kings 4:1

Some ministers are going to die and leave their ministries in debt. Most ministers are "married" to their ministries. The Elisha Church of the Double Portion will pay the debts of other ministries miraculously. Watch what happens!

> Elisha replied to her, "How can I help you? Tell me, what do you have in your house?" "Your servant has nothing there at all," she said, "except a little oil." (Oil represents the anointing.)
>
> Elisha said, "Go around and ask all your neighbors for empty jars (empty vessels). Don't ask for just a few.
>
> 2 Kings 4:2,3

The head man will die, and there will be just a little oil (a little anointing) left in that ministry. We who remain in this next generation are going to have to find all the empty vessels, vessels who have lost their anointing, joy, passion, and love. Vessels devoid of God and devoid of His gifts and of vision. We will find vessels that have no guile or sin in them. Vessels that are pure but empty.

> Then go inside and shut the door behind you and your sons. Pour oil into all the jars, and as each is filled, put it to one side.
>
> 2 Kings 4:4

We will pour a little bit of that anointing in every "jar" we can find as God miraculously stretches it. Yes, we will begin to anoint every empty vessel. One by one, little by little, and vessel by vessel until

God's people everywhere are filled to overflowing with the glory of that double portion. God will not let it run out until we are finished.

> She left him and afterward shut the door behind her and her sons. They brought the jars to her and she kept pouring. When all the jars were full, she said to her son, "Bring me another one." But he replied, "There is not a jar left." Then the oil stopped flowing.
>
> She went and told the man of God, and he said, "Go, sell the oil and pay your debts. You and your sons can live on what is left."
>
> 2 Kings 4:5,7

When they bring the empty vessels to us, we are to keep on pouring. Although we only have a little bit to start with, we are to keep on pouring until all the jars are full. Then we will look around for other empty vessels. That is what God is going to do in His next mighty outpouring. I would not miss it for anything.

That is why I tell my church, "This is not the time for giving up. It is time for holding on. This is not the time for looking back. This is a time to be strong."

When that time comes, of course it does not mean that we are to "sell" the oil in a literal sense. But I believe that when the anointing, the oil of God, is really on us and the vessels are really being filled, ministries will not have to go on television to beg and plead for money. Finances will come in supernaturally because of the oil. People will be anxious to give when their lives are being supernaturally changed and charged up for service to the Lord.

God is going to give this new Church supernatural power in the financial realm. When the prophet has died and his wife or ministry is left with very little anointing and no money to pay the bills, and when creditors threaten to take over and sell everything, those with the anointing will step in by the power of God and know exactly what to do. God is going to miraculously pay the debts so that the Church of Jesus will not be crippled in the sight of the world. We will be able to do exploits for God debt-free and with money to spare.

A Spirit of Debt

The Lord has shown me in the spirit that some ministries in great debt will resort to consulting witches. I saw a frightening vision one night of preachers with a Bible in one hand and a pistol in the other, not knowing which to use. The Lord showed me men under so much stress they were about to explode or have nervous breakdowns. They are losing everything, and the devil is going to try to come in and cause them to do things they should not.

Oral Roberts brought out a very profound point at the 1988 Charismatic Bible Ministries Conference in Tulsa. He talked about a "spirit of debt" which has fastened itself upon many people, ministries included. In our own church, we have realized that many people with financial problems do not have a spirit of poverty hanging over them but a spirit of debt.

Few Christians today are impoverished. Most live above the poverty level, but there is a spirit of debt that has gotten on us: credit cards, mortgages, cars, clothes, and debt, debt, debt. It is a spirit that really clouds us over and is painful. The Church of the Double Portion will kick out that spirit of debt and bring things to life again.

Bringing Things Back to Life

In the last part of Second Kings 4, Elisha ministered to a well-to-do woman who had lost her son. The Shunammite woman had built the prophet a shelter, a little room of his own on the roof of her house. She had constructed for him a "penthouse" where he could rest and break his travels as he passed her way.

The well-to-do will be drawn to those of the Church of the Double Portion. They will provide shelters and coverings. What is going to attract them to us is when they will have desperate needs for things that money cannot buy. And when that happens, miracles are going to take place for them through God's people.

> **He went in, shut the door on the two of them and prayed to the Lord. Then he got on the bed and lay upon the boy, mouth to mouth, eyes to eyes, hands to hands. As he stretched himself out upon him, the boy's body grew warm.**
>
> **2 Kings 4:33,34**

We are going to have to actually "lay our bodies" on the bodies of other churches, ministries, and ministers who are dead — eyes to eyes, mouth to mouth, hand to hand, and pray. We cannot disassociate ourselves from the dead ones. We have to help them recover life. We are going to recover the lost miracles and blessings. We are going to embrace the dead dreams and visions of people. Dead answers to prayer will be resurrected. We are going to cause life to re-enter them. What a glorious future awaits those who will see, hear, and respond to what the prophetic voice of God is saying to His Church!

The Sound of a Heavy Rain

After three and one-half years of drought and famine in Israel, God spoke to Elijah that finally it would rain. Elijah indicated his witness from the Lord when he told Ahab, **Go, eat and drink, for there is the sound of a heavy rain** (1 Kings 18:41).

The Hebrew word for *sound* as used in this passage is the same as the word translated other places as voice or *proclamation*. In other words, God spoke to Elijah deep in his spirit and told him the years of drought were over. The Lord had spoken, and that was all Elijah needed to start looking for the first cloud.

While Elijah went to pray on Mount Carmel where his last miracle had been performed, he sent his servant to look westward toward the sea for any indication of a change in weather conditions, or a sign of the changing of the season.

Then **Elijah climbed to the top of Mount Carmel, bent down to the ground and put his face between his knees** (1 Kings 18:42). His posture in prayer was a position of travail as if he was birthing a child. This posture was typical of a woman giving birth in eastern cultures. Notice that Elijah went back to the place where the fire had just fallen and burned up his sacrifice during the trial of faith with Jezebel's prophets. (1 Kings 18:16-40.) However, this time instead of praying for fire, he prayed for rain.

The King James Version of Zechariah 10:1 reads:

> **Ask ye of the Lord rain in the time (season) of the latter rain.... .**

228

The Full Expression of Joy

The coming revival will bring complete and full expression of joy. This means the presence of God will be more fully manifested both in the Church and in the world than at any other time in history. Psalm 16:11 says:

> You have made known to me the path of life; you will *fill me with joy in your* presence, with eternal pleasures at your right hand.

As I have said before, to many the presence of God will cause terror and paralyzing fear because of the sin and rebellion in them. But to those of us who eagerly await His return (Gal. 5:5), and who are praying even now in anticipation of the changing seasons, it will be a time of unspeakable joy with uncontrollable laughter and dancing in His presence.

One other point about praying in the will of God, based on His prophetic voice in your heart, is found in the book of Daniel.

> In the first year of his (Darius son of Xerxes) reign, I, Daniel understood from the Scriptures, according to the word of the Lord given to Jeremiah the prophet, that the desolation of Jerusalem would last seventy years. So I turned to the Lord God and pleaded with him in prayer and petition, in fasting, and in sackcloth and ashes.
>
> Daniel 9:2,3

A Five-Fold Flavor of Prayer

In this passage, Daniel recognized the time for a providential change in Israel's history. His recog-

229

nition was based upon the *scriptures* and the *prophetic words* of Jeremiah. The seventy-year captivity had expired, and Daniel was anxious for God to move. Daniel's *first* response to becoming aware of the prophecy was to pray. Actually, there were five expressions of prayer.

The first flavor of Daniel's prayer was the most common kind — *to entreat or to intercede* as if before a judge or a magistrate. This prayer represents regard, respect, or reverence for the solemnity of God. In reality, it was a form of worship and praise, a form of esteem for Jehovah Yahweh. All prayers should begin that way.

The second flavor of Daniel's prayer was *petition* or supplication. That means an intense, earnest asking; in other words, a petition is based on *faith*. James said the **effectual fervent prayer of a righteous man availeth much** (James 5:16 KJV).

The writer of the book of Hebrews said:

> **And without faith it is impossible to please God, because anyone who comes to him** (in prayer or otherwise) **must believe that he exists and that he rewards those who *earnestly* seek him.**
> **Hebrews 11:6**

The third flavor of Daniel's prayer was *fastings* that represented humility. (**I humbled my soul with fasting** — Ps. 35:13 KJV.) Fasting dramatizes the sincerity of your prayers, and represents acquiescence, surrender, and yielded obedience. Fasting reduces carnality and elevates the mind into the spirit of God.

The fourth flavor was *sackcloth*. Throughout the Bible, sackcloth is used as a symbol of mourning and brokenness. In effect, sackcloth symbolizes repentance and contrition of heart. Psalm 51:17 says, **...a broken and contrite heart, O God, you will not despise.** As we approach this mighty outpouring of God's holy presence and power, we need to remain penitent and sorry for our sins. Daniel's prayer was aflame with the purifier of sincere repentance.

The fifth, and final, flavor of Daniel's prayer was *ashes*. In Scripture, ashes frequently are associated with dust, and dust represents the flesh, or our earthly or carnal nature. Ashes remind us of our human vulnerability. They remind us of death. However, death also is a positive experience representing transition or renewal. To the saints, revival, restoration, and regeneration always follow death. As we go through the death and burial of our carnal and sinful nature, we rise to newness of life and eternal bliss. (Is. 61:3.)

A Time for Prophetic Praying

My point is to stress the importance and necessity of prophetic praying at this time in history. Spiritual prayers are prophetic prayers, and prophetic prayers are always and only in the Holy Spirit and by the will of God. Elijah on Mount Carmel with his head bowed was in a posture of prophetic praying. This kind of praying is long overdue among God's people, but it is on the rise again among those who hear the sound (the voice) of God's abundant rain.

Elijah sent his servant to look with his eyes for what the prophet heard with his spirit. At first, the servant saw nothing — which is often the case when God initially speaks. When God first speaks to me, there may be no outward sign of what I inwardly feel or hear. That is when faith must go to work in my heart.

When Elijah's servant returned the seventh time, he reported, **"A cloud as small as a man's hand is rising from the sea"** (1 Kings 18:44). That was the only sign Elijah needed. To most of us, that little cloud would have been much too insignificant to consider as really from God. Elijah was not like that. He already had received the witness in his spirit. He was travailing before God in prayer and fully expected the major outpouring of rain signaled by that small cloud.

Like Elijah, I can sense something on the horizon. I, too, can hear in my spirit "the sound of a heavy rain." Bondage and captivity to sin and disgrace is ending. The Feast of Tabernacles is now upon us, and the inexpressible joy God commands us to experience during that feast is just around the corner.

Yes, the storm clouds are gathering in the western skies, but prayer also is going forth on the eastern mountains. When west (promise) meets east (prayer and expectation), the lightning will flash and the thunder will roll across this universe, and the glory of the Lord will fill the earth. Oh, yes, I see the cloud!

The cloud about the size of a man's hand is something I have pictured in my mind many times. I see it as an open-palmed hand with the fingers stretched out and spread equally apart. I see that "hand" as representing the five-fold ministry of the Church.

Ephesians 4:11,12 says:

> **It was he (Jesus) who gave some to be apostles, some to be prophets, some to be evangelists, and some to be pastors and teachers, to prepare God's people for works of service, ...**

Notice that Jesus placed those "gifts" from Himself, or those offices, *in the Church*. The cloud Elijah's servant saw was a picture-prophecy of the New Testament Church of the Five-fold Ministry ushering in the last great revival before the Second Coming of Jesus.

The Fingers of God

About five years ago, I went skiing for the first time with a couple of friends from my college days. We went to Vail, Colorado, the day after Christmas, in one of the coldest winter seasons I ever remember. There was more than sixty inches of snow on the ground, and needless to say, the powder was threatening but inviting as well.

The entire trip was quite a challenge to me as a skiing novice, and my buddies were at least semi-pros. Too proud to slow them down or compete with their expertise, I sent them to the mountain slopes while I went through the rigors of the beginners' class.

By the end of the day I could hardly breathe, let alone talk, so I ended up having a lot of time to think and hear from God. While standing in the long ski lift lines waiting to return to the top of the mountain, I would take off my gloves, pull my fingers into the palms of my hands, and stick my hands underneath my outer garments to try to thaw out my fingers.

One of those times, while I was standing in line with my hands balled up and thrust into my chest, the Holy Spirit began to speak to me. This is what he said, "The fingers of God are chilly, too." (I thought immediately of the five-fold ministry.)

He continued, "I, too, am balling up my fingers warming them in the palm of my hand, thrusting them deep into my bosom and bringing them out occasionally to blow my living breath upon them to thaw them out for renewed use."

In the past, you have seen the fingers of God at work in the history of the Church. The *apostolic* movement of the first century (thumb), which really touches all the ministry offices; then the *prophetic* movements (forefinger), sporadically in operation over the past two thousand years; then the *evangelistic* ministries (the middle finger) — in other words, the Wesleys, Finney, Billy Sunday and Billy Graham, Oral Roberts, and others; then the *pastoral* ministries (the ring finger of commitment) from the first century to the mega-church pastors of modern times; and finally, the *teachers* (the small finger), digging in to find those hidden truths so often overlooked.

We have seen the fingers of God in separate and isolated operation many times during the years since the days of the Apostle Paul, but the Spirit of God showed me that in this next great wave of God's visitation, we will not see just one of His fingers in operation. We will see the entire hand of God sweeping the whole earth touching and handling every sovereign aspect of His kingdom and advancing His gospel to every creature on the globe.

Conclusion:
Prayer Marks a Turning Point

As I said at the beginning of this book, the Church of Jesus Christ has been at a place in history where spiritual roads or paths intersect. If God did not intervene at these crossroads, His Church would not be able to distinguish His signals from those of the enemy. I believe it will not be too much longer before this crisis will be over, and the flow of spiritual traffic will be resumed. God is about to restore the signs and wonders of the Church. His signs and wonders constitute His signature autographing and endorsing our lives and ministries for His glory and for His name's sake.

In the summer of 1988, the Lord spoke to my heart that the *major* shaking was over and no lasting damage had occurred to the foundations of His Church. Paul wrote to Timothy:

> Nevertheless, God's solid foundation stands firm, sealed with the inscription, "The Lord knows those who are his," and "Everyone who confesses the name of the Lord must turn away from wickedness.
>
> 2 Timothy 2:19

Although there is no damage to the foundation, for His Church is founded on Jesus, there has been a severe weakening. The Lord shows me that the aftershocks or the tremors following the main earthquake will cause the final collapse of ministries who refuse to restore *their* foundations through prayer, repentance, and allowing the Holy Spirit to evaluate their purposes, plans, and goals.

God said that He Himself would pull the plug on every ministry or spiritual leader who is spiritually dead.

He said, "All ministries or ministers who do not or cannot exist solely by My Holy Spirit will not survive these changing times."

Three Areas of Sin

While reading this book, if you have received a revelation from the Holy Spirit concerning sin in your life or ministry — no matter what it is or how large or small — then you need to repent and get rid of that thing. As you can see from the problems revealed in this book, there are three main areas of sin in the Church today, just as the Word says in First John 2:16:

> **For everything in the world — the cravings of sinful man, the lust of his eyes and the boasting of what he has and does — comes not from the Father but from the world.**

The *King James Version* calls those three areas **the lust of the flesh, and the lust of the eyes, and the pride of life.** In modern times, we might call these: lusts of the body, such as sex, food, or alcohol and drugs; lust of the eyes — money and possessions, including clothes; and power over others. We *could* call them immorality, greed, and ambition.

If you have found in yourself roots or full-blown plants in any of these areas, *and you want to be a part of the Church of the Double Portion*, you need to repent and turn away from those ungodly ways, desires, and attitudes. Pray along the lines of the following suggested prayers, or let the Holy Spirit lead you in a prayer from your heart.

1. Prayer for lusts of the flesh:

Heavenly Father,

Forgive me for my sins of immorality. Jesus is my example, and He never stooped to sins of the flesh. He never succumbed to the ways of the world. He laid aside His divinity and walked as a man to show us that it is possible to follow Your ways and do Your will and not fall into the things of the flesh.

Through the name of Jesus and by the power of the Holy Spirit, I set my will to live a clean and holy life. I renounce the things of the flesh. I renounce immorality. I renounce appetites that have allowed my body to rule my life. I set myself to turn immediately from any hint of fleshly sins, from eating too much to fornication. I desire to be a part of Your Body that is without spot or blemish.

With the help of Your Holy Spirit, I commit to live a morally blameless life.

2. Prayer for lusts of the eyes:

Heavenly Father,

Forgive me for lusting after money and possessions of any kind. I repent of falling into the sin of covetousness, whether it was in wanting to "keep up" with other people, or whether it was simply coveting the things of the world. Father, I realize that covetousness is a form of idolatry, and I repent that things have become an idol to me. I agree with Paul and Timothy, who wrote to the Colossians:

> **Put to death, therefore, whatever belongs to your earthly nature: sexual immorality, impurity, lust, evil desires and greed, which is idolatry. Because of these, the wrath of God is coming.**
> **Colossians 3:5,6**

Forgive me for not being a good steward of the money or property entrusted to me. I repent for having more love for myself than for You. First Corinthians 4:2 says that stewards are required to be found trustworthy. Lord, I want to be found faithful when You return or when I come to meet You.

3. Prayer for pride of life:

Heavenly Father:

Forgive me for highmindedness and a lust for power or a lust for status. Forgive me for using Your glory to build my name and not Your name. Forgive me for wanting the fame of this world. I have decided that I want my reward in the world to come rather than in this world. Help me learn humility before You and before my fellow Christians.

4. Prayer for shepherds who have misused their office:

Heavenly Father:

Forgive me for acting like a hireling instead of a true shepherd. Forgive me for beating the sheep in word or in deed. Forgive me if I have intentionally, or unintentionally, fleeced the sheep for my own benefit. Forgive me if I have not hunted the strays, delivered those in bondage, or healed those who were wounded in body, soul, or spirit. Father, I submit my will to Yours and commit to be the kind of shepherd You have called me to be.

If you have never become a child of God, if your hope is not yet in Jesus and you want to find Him, pray this prayer:

Heavenly Father,

I confess with my mouth that Jesus is Lord, and I believe in my heart that You raised Him from the dead. (Rom. 10:9,10.) I confess that without Jesus there is no hope for me, and I receive by faith the payment made for my sins by His blood. (Rom. 3:25.) I thank You, Lord, for Your forgiveness, and I forgive anyone who has ever offended me or that I thought committed an offense against me. (Matt. 6:9-14.) His blood cleanses me from all unrighteousness, and I know from Your Word that my sins will be remembered by You no more, that You have washed me whiter than snow. (Is. 1:18.) If I trust in You, I will never be put to shame. (Rom. 10:11.) I believe in Jesus; therefore, I have eternal life and will not perish. (John 3:16-18.)

I *do* believe with all my heart that the days to come, after God has finished His shaking and the separating of the wheat from the tares, will be the best days in the history of the Church. In spite of the hard things God has shown me and that I have shared in this book, I am very optimistic about the Church. I hope that you, like me, will decide to allow the Lord to purge everything out of your life that smacks of the flesh or of the soul in order that you also may be part of the 21st century Church. Get your life right with God, then claim your part of the double portion!

Yes, we are in a crisis, and we are at a crossroads, but the signs and flashing signals say the emergency vehicles of God's Holy Ghost paramedics are on the scene to administer the kind of spiritual care the Church needs to get us back on our feet and flowing in divine health, divine happiness, and divine holiness! Amen!

Truly, the best is yet to come!

 **Carlton Pearson** pastors one of the fastest growing churches in Tulsa, Oklahoma — Higher Dimensions. Started in 1981 as a storefront gathering of 75 people, today it is a multi-faceted ministry. During worship services 5,800 adults are ministered to weekly. In addition, over 1,000 children and teens receive ministry geared to their specific needs.

The congregation of Higher Dimensions is composed of many ages, races and cultures. One newspaper called it "a sociologist's fantasy, a compilation of people from every socio-economic class . . . a racial melting pot." Rev. Pearson prefers to call it "a stew." He places a high priority on family and country, reflected in his first television special, entitled: "America, We Love You."

Rev. Pearson serves on the board of regents at Oral Roberts University, as well as on the boards of several Christian missionary organizations. He has authored a variety of books and booklets carrying the message of deliverance: that Jesus Christ came to forgive the sins of all men and save their souls.

To contact Carlton Pearson, write:

P.O. Box 700007 • Tulsa, OK 74170

Additional copies of *Crisis at the Crossroads* are available from your local bookstore or from:

Dmetrius Publishing
P. O. Box 700007 • Tulsa, OK 74170